# ROGUE JUSTICE

WHEN YOU'RE RIGHT, YOU FIGHT

## STEVE NEAL

ROGUE JUSTICE

Copyright © 2025 by Steven R. Neal. All rights reserved.

No part of this publication may be reproduced, stored in a retrieval system, or transmitted, in any form or by any means, electronic, mechanical, photocopying, recording, or otherwise, without the prior written permission of the author, except as permitted under the 1976 United States Copyright Act.

ISBN: 979-8-9909631-4-6

This publication is sold with the understanding that the author is not engaged in rendering legal or professional services. If legal or policy advice is prudent, the reader should seek competent assistance in that area.

Although the stories in this book are based on true incidents, some of the details may have been changed.

# What People are Saying About _Rogue Justice_

In writing this review of **Rogue Justice**, I feel it necessary to establish my bona fides as a Rogue Justice Warrior. I served as a police officer from 1983 until 2005. I served in several capacities in the active Army, USAR, National Guard, and full-time National Guard from 1980 until 2022. I retired as a Police Lieutenant and served with Steve Neal, the last time in 2000-2001 as his lieutenant at the police academy. During my career in law enforcement, I served in a multitude of assignments and specialties and was twice decorated for valor in shootouts with armed criminals. In the military, I served nearly 30 years as a Green Beret and retired as a Chief Warrant Officer 5. I received the Silver Star medal and the Bronze Star Medal with Valor device for my actions in combat in Iraq in 2006 while serving as a Special Forces Warrant Officer and assistant detachment commander. I have never been one to run from the sounds of gun fire. I have always run straight to it. I have chosen to surround myself with those of the same mindset. A Rogue Justice Warrior is someone who always stands up for what is right, often at their own peril – be it physical, emotional, spiritual, personal, financial, or professional. In Iraq, whenever we faced an ambush from the enemy, the first thing I would say was, "Oh Hell no!" followed by GrimMagic 80 this is GrimMagic 84, Contact, Contact, Contact. Enemy contact was 38S…".

In 2010, a Major General told me, "You know what your problem is Chief? You take 'no' for an answer. Stop taking no for an answer." Much to the consternation of many Colonels and Command Sergeants Major, I quit taking no for an answer. And when I did, positive things happened for my unit and the Soldiers in it, and positive things happened for those I challenged to get to that 'yes' answer. I spent both of my careers in public service with two maxims: "Do what needs to be done;" and "Lead, follow, or get the hell out of the way." Steve has captured the essence of the American Spirit in this book. I cannot make any higher recommendation, and I hope you will join us in becoming Rogue Justice Warriors.

## Jim Herring
Chesterfield County Police Department 1983-2005
U.S. Army, USAR, VA ARNG, NCARNG 1990-2022

\* \* \* \*

*Rogue Justice* is more than a book; it's a leadership call to arms. Steven R. Neal defines the "Rogue Justice Warrior" as a bold, principled leader who challenges injustice, takes smart risks, and refuses to back down.

Through influential case studies of history's disruptors—Harriet Tubman, Winston Churchill, Dr. Martin Luther King Jr., and more—Neal highlights that authentic leadership requires defying norms to create meaningful change. He masterfully explores the paradox of leadership, showing that great leaders balance defiance with discipline and charisma with grit.

*Rogue Justice* is a practical blueprint for those who refuse to settle for mediocrity. It inspires us to fight for what's right and equips us with the tools and strategies to do so effectively, no matter what the cost.

*Rogue Justice* is a must-read for leaders who are ready to step into the arena. It offers practical principles that can be applied in real-life leadership situations, making it a valuable resource for those who are bold enough to lead.

## Dr. York Kleinhandler
Green Beret, Keynote Speaker, Professor of Practice,
Ducibus Consulting, Inc.

\* \* \* \*

Great read! [***Rogue Justice***] made me think of how I have always looked at the term rogue, usually with a negative connotation. This book allowed me to understand how many people, who we look up to as heroes, were placed in situations in their lives that made them challenge the system that they saw as harmful to themselves and others.

Simply put, all of us [can] become a Rogue Justice Warrior when put in the right place, at the right time, to stand up for what we believe is right when knowing that there will be negative consequences for our actions.

**Rick Mormando**
Mormando & Associates, Retired law enforcement,
Adjunct Professor

\* \* \* \*

As I was reading [***Rogue Justice***], several images came to mind— John Wayne was one. The characteristics attributed to a *Rogue Justice Warrior* make [them] sound almost like a superhero. This closely aligns with **utilitarianism** and **consequentialism**, which prioritize achieving the greatest good for the greatest number. I enjoyed reading the justice case studies and the historical rogue protagonists.

**Teresa Hale**
Criminal Justice Faculty, ECPI University

\* \* \* \*

In **Rogue Justice**, readers are taken on an inspiring journey through the lives of individuals who have refused to bow to societal pressure, legal hurdles, or fear, standing firm in their beliefs to fight for justice. This book is not just a call to action—it is a celebration of resilience, courage, and the unwavering spirit of those who challenge the status quo for the greater good.

Mr. Neal masterfully weaves together real-life stories of Rogue Justice Warriors, individuals who have risked everything to stand up for what they believe in. What sets *Rogue Justice* apart is its balance between storytelling and philosophical reflection. It does not merely recount events; it delves into the psychological and moral strength required to take a stand when the odds seem insurmountable. The book challenges readers to reflect on their own convictions and whether they would have the courage to fight when justice is on the line. **"When you're right, you fight!"**

## Bradley Richmond, DC
Doctor of Chiropractic

\* \* \* \*

*Rouge Justice*, written by Steve Neal, is an excellent study in the characteristics and action of notable people who have stood up to conditions that try to defeat and control the thoughts and actions of people who are facing overwhelming adversity. It proves through their examples the results of those who chose to take the path of action that are morally and ethically correct to overcome the injustices. Steve's vast knowledge and expertise on this difficult subject is a book that could be used as a textbook for both the beginner and the experienced warrior.

## William G. Haneke, Captain , USA (Ret)
Published Author "Trust Not"
1966 USMA , 1975 VCU Healthcare and Business
 Administration
Co-Founder and President of Families of the Wounded Fund, Inc. 2005-2024

\* \* \* \*

"How rogue are you? That's the question posed by Steve Neal in the closing pages of *Rogue Justice*. Fortunately, this dynamic, heart-pounding account of the most outstanding men and women of our past and present will provide the answer to that all important question. Steve weaves the reader through history as he explains the characteristics and traits of the greatest amongst us, while teaching us along the way with real-life case studies and thought provoking insights on what it means and takes to be rogue. This is the book for a time such as this, just when we all needed it."

**Dr. Travis Yates, Author and Trainer**
The Courageous Police Leader
www.TravisYates.org

# ROGUE JUSTICE WARRIOR

THE WEAPONS WE FIGHT WITH
ARE NOT THE
WEAPONS OF THE WORLD.
2 COR. 10:4

# Dedication

***Rogue Justice*** is dedicated to my daughters, Brittany, and Ashton. I could not be any prouder of you than I am. You are smart, compassionate, hardworking, kindhearted, conscientious good citizens who do not hesitate to go rogue when you feel strongly about an issue. This makes me smile, as I know that you have learned your lessons well. The love, devotion, and guidance you show to my grandchildren fills my heart with pride and contentment. It is obvious that the future of our family is in good hands.

***Rogue Justice*** readers are fortunate to have benefitted from many hours of consultation, hard work, and know-how that friends contributed to this project. Without their willingness to share skills and expertise, this mission may have never been accomplished. A special appreciation is extended to Andrew Barefoot.

Thank you to my family, extended family, and close friends for the love and support you have shown to me through the years. Each of you are embedded deep in my soul, and I will always hold you close. My wish is that you experience success, happiness, and peace throughout your lifetime.

Lastly, I dedicate ***Rogue Justice*** to the preeminent country on earth, the United States of America. We have the good fortune of reaping many blessings provided by the greatest republic of all time. Founded for liberty and freedom, the original insurrectionist patriots were *warriors who went rogue, seeking justice!* They were willing to sacrifice their fortunes and their lives to achieve the goal. Thank you, Colonists and Founding Fathers, for teaching us that idealism, determination, unity, and readiness to fight are principles for establishing a society where all can pursue happiness and live free from oppression.

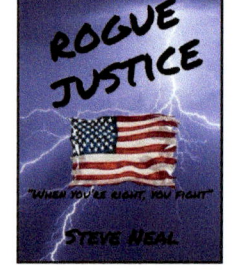

# Prologue

*Rogue Justice* embodies decisive, bold, and fearless action taken to nullify wrongs, abolish inequality, or invalidate injustice. A Rogue Justice Warrior acts according to a robust personal code of ethics, prioritizing the greater good over self. They rebelliously stand up for fairness regardless of consequences.

Bravery, fortitude, and fearlessness epitomize the Rogue Justice Warrior. Taking courageous action requires hutzpah. The principled and honorable rogue does not sidestep conflict, they battle audaciously when they believe in a cause. Righteous Rogue Justice Warriors refuse to allow fear to take away their voice.

Daring, resilience, and gallantry ooze from the Rogue Justice Warrior's pores. Frequently the guardian of civil liberty, they cherish combat when they feel that freedoms are at stake. They relish going outside the norm when necessary to drive needed, positive change.

Rogue Justice Warriors take smart, calculated risks, practice straight talk, and never panic. Their admirable patriotism, shrewdness, and charm, make them formidable opponents in every encounter.

Rogue leaders rely on the rumblings of gut instinct. They do hard things that need to be done. Because they stand up to disreputable exploits, Rogue Justice Warriors are true heroes! A Rogue Justice Warrior lives the creed **"When You're Right, You Fight."**

# Foreword

When my friend Steve reached out to tell me that he had written a new book, I figured it was an update or reworking of his must read "***Toxic Boss Blues***" which every law enforcement officer in every agency around the world needs to read. Steve devoted his life to public service and, while I no longer work as a police officer, I will always be a cop. I have also shared that book with countless friends, both in law enforcement and the civilian world.

I was not sure what new twist my friend would have on those issues but I was anxious to see. In fact, I asked him what he would be diving into with a TBB sort of book. No Jeff, it is not that at all he said. It's about going rogue, rogue justice in fact. Now I was puzzled. After all, why would my friend, a cop's cop want to write about rogues? Like most of us, I immediately characterized a rogue as a bad guy. When you go rogue, you look at society's rules and make a conscious decision to ignore them. Honest people work hard, rogues, well they find a different way to go about generating income. I was truly baffled by Steve's desire to write about those folks who are rogues.

After reading this book, I realized that Steve was on to something so much bigger than I had imagined. Oh, and my entire perception was wrong! Steve reminded me that the real definition of rogue is not criminal nor is it dishonest. It is simply about not following the established rules. I started to understand what he meant by rogue justice. As you explore the book you will see why Steve quotes Chief Sitting Bull who said that "Warriors are not always what you think of as warriors."

Our view of the rogue is usually negative but Steve is not talking about the pickpocket. He is speaking of, as he describes them, "rogue justice warriors" among us. The rogue justice warrior has an inherent strength and courage rooted in his or her understanding of what is right. What must be protected, defended, and strengthened. They embody a unique set of strengths and common traits. Their internal compass is pointed north and they know it as surely as they know their name. The rogue justice warrior is surely found in the ranks of the military and first responders but they can also be found in every other part of our community. Your child's teacher might be a rogue justice warrior. So too, your faith leader could be a rogue justice warrior. Hopefully those in positions of national leadership embody that which makes a rogue justice warrior a true rogue justice warrior. Steve does a far better job than I can in describing what goes in to the DNA of the rogue justice warrior. Courage is essential. The courage to know what is truly right. The courage to clearly articulate that knowledge. Finally, the courage to fight to make things right, no matter the personal costs. The rogue justice warrior does not sit quietly and passively on the sidelines of life, seeing wrong being committed but saying nothing. The rogue justice warrior suits up and gets in the game to make things right. Ephesians 6:10 - 18 speaks of the full armor of God. Every rogue justice warrior has been outfitted with the Belt of truth, Breastplate of righteousness, Shoes of the gospel of peace, Shield of faith, Helmet of salvation and Sword of spirit. When wearing the full armor of God, the rogue justice warrior can do only one thing and that is seek justice in its purest form, especially rogue justice. Rogue justice is pursued by that rogue justice warrior even as others are standing aside. Justice must be attained even when you are facing overwhelming odds. We all know that but few of us act on it in the way that the rogue justice warrior does. Carefully read the following accounts of rogue justice warriors. Right now, you may not think that Jesus, Harriet Tubman, Crazy Horse, Martin Luther King Jr., and Donald J. Trump have much in common. Steve Neal skillfully will disabuse the notion that the people he writes about are simply interesting, not just random players in life. Through the prism of a skilled investigator and brilliant writer he shows us what characteristics bind these rogue justice warriors together. While each lives in different times with different problems, each one ultimately fights for what is right without regard to the potential ills that could befall them. As you read these stories of rogue justice warriors, see which strengths you have. In every society, in every time period, and in every locale, there are rogue justice warriors. You might be the very rogue justice warrior who will be called upon to fight for what is right.

# Jeff Katz
Author, Certified Mental Health Coach and Certified Professional Speaker

# Rogue Justice!
*"Now More Than Ever"*

## Table of Contents

| | | |
|---|---|---|
| Chapter 1: | Rogue Justice Warrior DNA | 1 |
| Chapter 2: | Warrior in the Arena | 8 |
| Chapter 3: | Guts – Courage in the Face of Adversity | 15 |
| Chapter 4: | Opposites and Paradoxes | 25 |
| Chapter 5 | Justice | 32 |
| Chapter 6: | Historic Rogue Protagonists: | 41 |
| | Jesus | 43 |
| | Harriet Tubman | 48 |
| | General George Patton | 51 |
| | Crazy Horse | 55 |
| | Dr. Martin Luther King, Jr. | 59 |
| | Sir Winston Churchill | 64 |
| | President Donald J. Trump | 68 |
| | More Rogues | 72 |
| Chapter 7: | *When You're Right, You Fight* | 74 |
| Chapter 8: | Things you Might Hear a Rogue Justice Warrior Say | 86 |
| Chapter 9: | Rogueometer | 88 |
| Conclusion | | 97 |
| About the Author | | 98 |
| Sources and Credits | | 100 |

# Chapter 1

## *ROGUE JUSTICE WARRIOR DNA*

### COMMON ROGUE PERCEPTIONS

The term *Rogue* has been used to refer to a type of human scoundrel since at least the 15th century. A rogue villain exhibited erratic, dangerous, uncontrollable, often criminal behavior. Old time rogues operated at the boundaries of humanity. Rogues were habitually described as adroit at trickery, yet stealth in their methodology. Skillful at avoiding direct confrontation, the success of a rogue was thought to be dependent upon their elevated ability to ensure that their deception remained undetected.

Early rogues have been depicted as rascals with questionable mores. Egocentric, rogues were frequently portrayed as tricksters who made unsavory, selfish choices. Illegitimate, fraudulent, chicanery was thought to be their standard operating procedure. Lacking virtue, the charlatan rogue manipulated situations by employing their illicit charm. They exploited vulnerable situations, caused harm to others, and undermined social order.

History recounts many well-known rogues who have used unethical traits and actions to facilitate abuse of power. Just a few who personify depraved rogue behaviors include Caligula, Machiavelli, Adolf Hitler, Benito Mussolini, and Jim Jones. Nasty, cruel, and wicked rogues use dishonorable, greedy, self-serving tactics based on fear, hate, and intimidation. Anti-heroic rogues represent the exact opposite traits and behaviors of the praiseworthy and respectable Rogue Justice Warriors discussed throughout this book.

### ALTERNATIVE WAY TO LOOK AT ROGUE BEHAVIOR

Certainly, some behavior categorized as rogue can be viewed as less than desirable. If being a rogue and demonstrating rogue behavior have such negative connotations and influence, why would anybody contend otherwise? The work that follows will help the reader understand how appropriately going rogue is often necessary, *even essential*, to extraordinarily successful outcomes.

Resolution of difficult situations call for diverse solutions. Good leaders easily adapt the application of various styles and methods of intervention to whatever dilemma they encounter. Seems likely that we can all agree that there are times when a catalyst must break from conventional wisdom to get the job done. In the face of contemptable interference, great trailblazers must be able to think quickly and impose creative solutions that mitigate the depth of significant opposition.

In this introductory chapter, we will discover that rogue behavior does not always grade out as negative. In fact, Rogue Justice Warriors persistently display virtuous qualities and performance. As we shall see later in **Rogue Justice**, many of the most audacious architects of the world's greatest successes use what we will come to know as Rogue Justice Warrior behavior to facilitate spectacularly superior outcomes.

## **DNA OF A ROGUE JUSTICE WARRIOR**

Examination into what it means to be a Rogue Justice Warrior includes this focus: *Who is a Rogue Justice Warrior?* This analysis shines a spotlight upon convictions, beliefs, traits, and characteristics that help explain the intrinsic anatomy of Rogue Justice Warrior superstars. Equally important will be this examination: *What do Rogue Justice Warriors do?* This section will help identify dexterous leadership behaviors that are involved with outcomes of excellence.

Successful Rogue Justice Warriors (RJW) are unquestionably distinguished leaders. They routinely demonstrate their intelligence, good judgment, problem-solving ability, and servant mindset. Hardworking and smart, they hold themselves accountable. Yet, there is much more depth to a Rogue Justice Warrior.

The following bullet points illuminate tangible rogue qualities and behaviors that elevate Rogue Justice Warrior performance to an elite echelon.

Note that the following attributes are commonly and consistently found in Rogue Justice Warriors. There may be some deviation in the density and intensity of individual warrior characteristics and activities. The level of variance regarding Rogue Justice Warrior behaviors and attributes will be explored in depth in Chapter 9, when we test individual levels of rogueness.

Rogue Justice Warrior DNA includes:

- <u>Mental Toughness</u>

    **Traits**: Iron-willed, rugged, decisive, tenacious, resolute, bold, composed, strong character, emotionally confident

    **Behaviors**: Unfazed when making hard decisions; digs deep, manages emotions, and tackles tough tasks head-on; strong willed, does whatever needs to be done regardless of circumstances or consequences; fortified and committed; an unshakeable sense of itinerary and command helps stay the course even when the going gets tough; unwilling to yield to pressure, takes a stand against injustice or inequity even when others will be displeased; makes cool-headed, sound, confident decisions; fierce competitor and fearsome opponent.

- <u>Gutsy</u>

    **Traits**: Risk taker, inner strength, fortitude, confident, tough, daring, brave, fearless, undaunted, stouthearted

    **Behaviors**: Takes smart, measured gambles when they see potential for a huge payoff; routinely steady during a crisis; makes exceptional decisions on the fly, and relishes rowing against the tide; willing to wade into danger simply because they see a need that demands action; exudes an aura of daring and conviction that others can see, feel, and almost taste; charts the course, speaks up, and executes without fear; not afraid to take risks, takes the lead.

- *Believes in Themself*

    **Traits**: Self-trust, confident, secure, poised, self-assured, definite, calm, self-possessed, certain, self-confident

    **Behaviors**: Strong belief and trust in their ability; has the courage to trust their own instincts; faces challenges with confidence, and pursues goals without being swayed by doubt; stays focused when things get tough; demonstrates a grounded assurance in what can be accomplished; inspire others with their contagious confidence; an undeniable sense of self-worth drives them, allowing bold decision-making, calculated risks, and learning from disappointments; their belief in themselves makes them both resilient and proactive; Sees obstacles as opportunities to grow.

- *Decisive*

    **Traits:** Clearsighted, strong-minded, resolute, authoritative, focused, strong-minded, purposeful, definitive, firm, clear thinking

    **Behaviors**: Makes the tough call without hesitation; quick and confident decision-maker, inspires followership; decisions are customarily viewed as correct; analytical thinker who leverages strength and focus; triangulates data and frames message so that it resonates with diverse groups; able to break components into small, understandable, manageable parts; proves to be the right person for the right job at the right time.

- *Conscientious*

    **Traits**: Meticulous, just, respectable, upright, worthy, ethical, principled, impartial, thorough, evenhanded, hard-working, reliable

    **Behaviors**: Acts according to a robust personal code of ethics; takes a stand against unfair practices and advocates for equality of outcome; prioritizes the greater good; take actions that align with their values; behaves in a way that is fair and compassionate; shows deference to individuals that earn their respect; takes responsibility for errors; Keeps promises and adheres to principles, especially when no-one is watching.

- *Rebellious*

    **Traits**: Disobedient, unruly, insubordinate, defiant, stubborn, revolutionary, militant, noncompliant, resistant

    **Behaviors**: Dissents against injustice; challenges authority and norms; provokes assumptions, and pushes boundaries; questions established ways of doing things, resists personal limitations and societal expectations; deliberately defies conventional wisdom, strays from prescribed procedures or protocols; righteously mutinous when necessary.

- *Courageous*

    **Traits**: Brave, bold, dauntless, heroic, audacious, unafraid, spirited, gallant, unflinching, brash, self-assured, nervy

    **Behaviors:** Not paralyzed by fear; does the right thing, speaks hard truths; faces anxiety, danger, or adversity with determination and inner strength; willing to stand up for what they believe; responds in a way that is true to their belief system; models professed values; is not deterred by challenges or risks; unafraid of consequences; is the first person in a crowd to rise to a challenge; makes arduous decisions; refuses to allow fear to take away their voice.

- *Charming*

    **Traits**: Confident, suave, captivating, charismatic, gracious, courteous, likable, smooth, polished, elegant, cultured, refined, enticing, tempting

    **Behaviors**: Displays likeable and engaging personality that attracts and delights; exudes self-assurance, but not arrogance; possesses a magnetic appeal that draws people close; displays warmth and genuine pleasantness; speech and manner are graceful; makes others feel at ease and comfortable in their presence; listens attentively.

- *Shrewd*

    **Traits**: Perceptive, discerning, cunning, clever, sharp-witted, crafty, astute, insightful, canny, sly, wily, crafty, guile

    **Behaviors**: Persuades others to their point of view; resourceful and clever, turns situations to their advantage; keen judgment allows canny, instantaneous, decision-making; reads between the lines; thinks several steps ahead, anticipating potential problems and opportunities; easily adapts to changing circumstances regardless of the situation; interprets situations, people, and purposes quickly; makes other feel as though it was their idea.

- *Authentic*

    **Traits**: Genuine, sincere, believable, down to earth, one of us, candid, real, true, straightforward

    **Behaviors**: Leads with the heart; does not need the limelight, but will use it to their advantage; actions are genuine and honest; statements and dealings leave no doubt that they are truly concerned about the welfare of others; passion is transparent, yet their language is plain-spoken; inspires trust with realism; performance is seen as the real deal; inspires others by being open, vulnerable, and by demonstrating an unwavering commitment to being true to themselves and their values.

- *Exceptional Communicator*

    **Traits:** Great listener, eloquent, persuasive, high interpersonal skill, diplomatic, emotional intelligence

    **Behaviors:** Adapts their communication style for the situation; efficiently reads verbal and non-verbal cues; excels at conveying ideas, information, and emotions in a clear, effective, and engaging manner; effectively relates to all audiences; creates a visceral connection with people by being empathetic, listening intently, and responding reflectively; asks good questions, uses silence as a tool, and demonstrates that they really care about people; keeps associates informed; gets others to buy into the message; makes people feel part of the process.

- *Hard No*

    **Traits:** Refuse, veto, deny, negative, reject, nope, no way, by no means, rebuff

    **Behaviors:** Strong and outright refusal, rejection of anything that goes against their belief system; formidably opposed to some ideas; will not be swayed to change their mind; value centric decisions are not open for negotiation, compromise, or reconsideration; decision is final and non-negotiable; unchangeable mental sturdiness; firmly and resolutely stands ground regardless of pressure; willing to take heat if stance is unpopular.

## **SUMMARY**

Conviction, talent, heart, and fortitude also play a huge role in the DNA of a Rogue Justice Warrior. The combination of RJW mentality, and execution of the extraordinary endeavors that they carry out, would not rise to the level of brilliance without the addition of an honorable spirit. The finest Rogue Justice Warriors have that certain something, an intangible moxie, which sets them apart from the norm. The strength of human zest; desire, boldness, and courageousness further assist in defining the makeup of a Rogue Justice Warrior.

Because Rogue Justice Warriors are fearless, they stand up for what they believe is right regardless of consequences. They are not swayed by outside pressure, they face challenges head on, and they stay true to themselves and their beliefs. Rogue Justice Warriors are willing to take risks when appropriate, and they recover quickly from setbacks. Rogue Justice Warriors are tenacious combatants who will attack relentlessly when they believe it essential.

# Chapter 2

## *WARRIOR IN THE ARENA*

*"The warrior, for us, is one who sacrifices himself for the good of others. His task is to take care of the elderly, the defenseless, those who cannot provide for themselves, and above all, the children"*

**Sitting Bull**
**Hunkpapa Lakota Sioux**

### WARRIOR DEFINED

To fully grasp the concepts found in **Rogue Justice**, we must first examine common definitions of what it means to be a warrior. Dictionary.com defines a warrior as "A person engaged or experienced in warfare; soldier, or, a person who shows or has shown great vigor, courage, or aggressiveness." Vocabulary.com expands this by stating that a warrior can be "Anyone who fights the good fight, whether in politics, or on the job." Similarly, Freedictionary.com describes a warrior as "One who is engaged aggressively or energetically in an activity, cause, or conflict."

### HISTORIC WARRIOR CULTURES

#### *Spartans*

The Spartans of ancient Greece, built a culture based upon the expectancy of military supremacy. At age 7, Spartan boys (except for firstborn sons) were enrolled in the Agoge. The Agoge was a rigorous training academy that set the tone for a lifetime of military proficiency and readiness. The

Phalanx-Insiderrelease.com

Agoge produced hardened recruits, who by age 20 formally transitioned to the role of soldier. Spartan soldiers were expected to remain in service until the age of 60.

Esprit de corps was a defining trait of the Spartan fighting force (history.com, 2009). Spartan warriors are most famously known for a battle tactic recognized as the phalanx. The phalanx required highly disciplined and synchronized maneuvering. Execution of the tactic in battle could only be accomplished following extensive, well-organized military practice. The Spartan military creed was rooted in discipline, endurance, and strength. (history.com, 2009).

### *Romans*

The ancient Roman Empire became one of the largest governed territories in the world thru conquest and assimilation of enemy lands. Rome's military was defined by professionalism, discipline, intricate organization, and relentless effectiveness (RomanEmpire-History.com, 2023).

The Roman military is credited with changing the nature of war. Devastating weapons, advanced tactics, and superior engineering gave the Romans a decisive edge. Though they suffered defeats, their unyielding resilience made them formidable. "If you beat them once, they always came back" (Elliot, Simon, 2018, HistoryHit.com). Their motivation extended beyond conquest—Rome had an insatiable appetite for wealth and territory, often integrating vanquished armies into their own ranks. Resilience and grit helped the Romans establish a culture of winning.

### *Assyrian Empire*

The Assyrian Empire is often considered the first superpower of the ancient world, (Jaras, Owen, 2016,). Spanning the fertile valleys of the Tigris and Euphrates rivers in

Wikimedia Commons

Mesopotamia, the Assyrian Empire was both the breadbasket of the ancient world and the birthplace of modern civilization. (Jaras, Owen, 2016)

The Assyrians employed a military culture and mindset that tied armed interest unequivocally to the affairs of the state and the public welfare. Newly discovered iron age technology enabled them to mass-produce superior weaponry (Jaras, Owen, 2016). They also pioneered the tactic of preemptive attack, using aggression as a form of defense (Jaras, Owen, 2016).

## *Vikings*

Jack Keay

While Viking raiding expeditions were infamous for their brutality, the Norse were also skilled nautical traders and colonizers. The continent of North America was visited by the Vikings long before Columbus landed in the Caribbean. (Goodrich, Ryan, 2016). The word Viking is drawn from the Scandinavian terms *Vikingr*, meaning someone who goes on expeditions, usually abroad, and Vikingar (Jesch, Judith, 2017).

The Vikings most certainly were a warrior society with the cultural ethos of violence and conflict written into their DNA. (Goodrich, Ryan, 2016). The communal and religious belief that the moment of death is preordained instilled a sense of reckless daring. Viking interpretation was that dying with fearlessness and glory was a worthwhile objective.

Vikings were known as Berserkers; professional warriors displaying trance-like engagement with the battle, often naked, and feigning lunacy. (Goodrich, Ryan, 2016). The psychological effect of berserkers leading an attacking force often had the enemy simply dropping their weapons and running. Those battles were won before they even began.

*Samurai*

The Samurai, whose name means "Those who serve," were Japan's warrior elite. Samurai combined military culture with religious ritual. An ideal samurai is a stoic warrior who follows an unwritten code of conduct. The code, known as Bushido, holds that bravery, honor, and personal loyalty are above life itself. Defeat, or dishonor often led to seppuku; ritual suicide by disembowelment (Britannica.com).

Samurai beliefs gradually worked their way into the Japanese government. A hereditary military dictatorship became known as a Shogun. Systematically, Shogun and Samurai became a fundamental knighthood of privileged elites. They practicing a stylized and heavily ritualized system of military and combat discipline. (historycollection.com). Zen Buddhism, an ideological system of austerity, simple ritual, and a belief that salvation comes from within, became the center of Samurai expression. (historycollection.com).

## **WARRIOR MINDSET FOUND IN AVERAGE CITIZENS**

The great Sioux chief, Sitting Bull, once remarked, "Warriors are not always what you think of as warriors." Being a warrior is about more than military combat. It is your authors strong belief that the populace warriors in every culture determine both the height and longevity of societal prolongation. Everyday citizen warriors must be tough, hard-edged, honorable persons. Battle tested, skilled in winning, tactically sophisticated, non-military pugilists, should be equally effective whether on offense or defense. As protectors and providers, every day civilian warriors have faith in themselves, and they never give up. They believe that they can overcome any challenge. Rogue Justice Warriors, whether military or civilian, refuse to be bullied into submission.

A soldier can be a Rogue Justice Warrior, but RJW's are also frequently found acting as good citizens. Readers should recognize that a Rogue Justice Warrior is anyone fighting honorably and valiantly for worthwhile purposes. One does not have be struggling for the last spot on Noah's Ark to personify a fiercely immersed combatant. When passionate about a topic, courage, pugnacity, and doggedness raises the level of the fight, and fuels the fierceness of the battle. Rogue Justice Warriors are talented scrappers, all in, they commit themselves with all their heart.

Rogue Justice Warriors bring ferocity, bravery, steadfastness, and dynamism to every battle. The combination of expertise, attitude, and fitting savagery means that RJW's stand a very high chance of emerging victorious. Betting against a Rogue Justice Warrior normally proves unwise.

## WHY A ROGUE JUSTICE WARRIOR WILL BE IN THE ARENA

In 1910, one year after he left the office of President, Theodore Roosevelt delivered his famous lecture *Citizenship in a Republic* in Sorbonne, France. Commonly known as the Man in the Arena speech, Roosevelt's remarks have inspired millions. The most often quoted portion of his speech is:

*"It is not the critic who counts; not the man who points out how the strong man stumbles, or where the doer of deeds could have done them better. The credit belongs to the man who is actually in the arena, whose face is marred by dust and sweat and blood; who strives valiantly; who errs, who comes short again and again, because there is no effort without error and shortcoming; but who does actually strive to do the deeds; who knows great enthusiasms, the great devotions; who spends himself in a worthy cause; who at the best knows in the end the triumph of high achievement, and who at the worst, if he fails, at least fails while daring greatly, so that his place shall never be with those cold and timid souls who neither know victory nor defeat."*

**Theodore Roosevelt**

The Man in the Arena message references those brave enough to be actively involved (participants) in dynamic activities and undertakings, despite the risk of failure or criticism. Roosevelt offered sharp criticism to those who point out how the strong man stumbles. He called the critic the one who does nothing but bring others down. This individual, Roosevelt said, "Was not fit as a citizen in a great democratic republic."

Roosevelt's remarks also point out that virtues like self-restraint, common sense, courage, and tenacity are paramount. He went on to say that "For a nation to be great, average citizens must pull their weight." Roosevelt preferred citizens who "Quell the storm and ride the thunder." He reminded us that "Those who have nobly ventured and put forth all their heart and strength" are the ones to be admired. "Even if they fail, they can take comfort in the fact that they followed their virtues. In this way, they have still succeeded."

By referencing the arena, Roosevelt evoked images of ancient Roman gladiators. Roman fighters were tough, frequently facing life-and-death situations. The gladiator represents an individual who is willing to take risks, confront hardship, and put themselves on the line. Perseverance, resilience, determination to get back up after being knocked down are crucial components underscoring the significance of civilian Rogue Justice Warriors. Gladiators understood that short-term failure was not necessarily their end since spectators in the coliseum could offer a gesture known as *pollice compresso* (hiding the thumb inside the fist) that could grant them another chance at survival (Smallwood, Karl, 2014).

## **ARENA: IMPACT ON ROGUE JUSTICE**

Rogue Justice Warriors understand that action, even in the face of failure, is more commendable than sitting on the sidelines. It is easy to criticize and judge others when we are not the one taking the risks. Rogue Justice Warriors, passionate about what they are doing, are driven by purpose and a sense of mission. Rogue Justice Warriors commit themselves to work that is meaningful, work that has the potential to make a difference. In everything that they do, they must be fully devoted, all the while ignoring the omnipresent noise. Rogue Justice Warriors are willing to battle through whatever comes their way, even when it means sacrificing personal comfort and well-being.

Rogue Justice Warriors use their voice and influence to impact their environment. Being in the arena includes vigorously expressing what needs to be declared. RJW's are not cowered by unease, trepidation, or intimidation. They never let fear silence what needs to be spoken. Private citizen Rogue Justice Warriors do not necessarily need to be public figures to be impactful. Being all-encompassing, actively engaged, part of the solution, is being enthusiastically in the arena.

The most effective, praiseworthy, Rogue Justice Warriors possess an indefinable grit and obstinacy which make them stand out in a crowd. The strength of gusto, yearning, brashness, and audaciousness help define the essence of a Rogue Justice Warrior. In a world that is increasingly complex, confusing, and unstable, we need Rogue Justice Warriors, *in the arena, now more than ever!*

Indeed, our survival as a nation depends upon the commitment of citizen Rogue Justice Warriors rising to the occasion. We need Rogue Justice Warriors ready to engage, to battle, to slay the dragon. Todd Beamer and his fellow airline passengers, showed us by example on 9-11, when they selflessly rallied a group of citizen heroes on that plane over Shanksville, Pennsylvania. They sacrificed their very existence to save the lives of strangers. *Well done, Todd Beamer and fellow Rogue Justice Warriors! Salute!*

Now, the question remains: Can your country count on you to step into the arena and lead? If not you, then who?

I appeal to you; commit now (this very second) to forever "Quelling the storm and riding the thunder" as Roosevelt said. Stand tall, strike hard, and fight with honor!

# Chapter 3

## *COURAGE IN THE FACE OF ADVERSITY – GUTS*

*"Courage is contagious. When a brave man takes a stand, the spines of others are often stiffened"*

**Billy Graham**

### UNAFRAID

Courage is a seminal attribute of the Rogue Justice Warrior! True courage is not the absence of fear, but the ability to act despite it. Courage is manifested by physical, moral, and emotional strength when facing apprehension, danger, or hardship. The trait is verified by being unafraid and resolute in the face of challenge. A courageous decision-maker upholds their values and principles even when they know that the stance they have taken involves risks and uncertainty. Courage is not just an instinct; it is an energizing force that propels bold action despite daunting obstacles.

Those who embody courage tackle life's difficulties with fortitude and vigor. Courage facilitates our ability to act despite perilous ambiguity. Mental strength and pluck facilitate the ability to recover from setbacks or failures. Courageous warriors use adversity as a catalyst for growth and learning. Mettle helps individuals bounce back from obstruction and keep moving forward despite seemingly insurmountable hurdles.

Courage is easy to discuss, harder to demonstrate. Courageous Rogue Justice Warriors rarely boast about their gallantry, preferring their actions to speak for them. Gutsy warriors serve as pioneers, setting a powerful example for friends, family, and community. Courage fosters a culture of heroism. Gutsy, courageous thoughts and deeds make high level accomplishment possible.

A Rogue Justice Warrior leads with their heart and soul. People naturally follow them, sensing something extraordinary. Non-warriors want to go along for the ride. Rogue Justice Warrior passion is infectious, their drive unwavering, and their intolerance for mediocrity is absolute. They do not merely endure challenges; they love to metaphorically give the difficult situation a firm kick in the rear.

## **NUTS AND BOLTS OF GUTSY COURAGENESS**

*A. Anxiety Management*: Acknowledging, confronting, and overcoming fear

*B. Willingness to act*: Choosing action despite fright, worry, or hesitation

*C. Exercising the Backbone*: Makes arduous, "character defining" choices

*D. Resolute Vigor*: Willpower and determination concerning strenuous decisions

*E. Confidence*: Unshakable self-trust and self-assurance

*F. Risk Taking*: Bold decision-making despite uncertainty

*G. Integrity*: Uncompromising adherence to principles and values

*H. Firm Boundaries- Reject*: Saying no when necessary

*I. Decisiveness*: Acting without hesitation. Unflinching

*J. Audaciousness*: Unapologetic, poised certainty

## ROGUE JUSTICE WARRIORS – COURAGEOUS AND GUTSY

Gutsy is a slang expression that suggests nerve, brashness, and the willingness to take risks and face difficult situations head-on. It implies a combination of determination, toughness, and inner strength. A gutsy individual is fearless, daring, and unafraid to confront obstacles or make difficult decisions. Gutsy people are at their best when the risks are high and the outcome is uncertain or potentially dangerous.

Gutsy Rogue Justice Warriors personify valor, resilience, and a no-nonsense attitude in the face of adversity. Being spirited and gutsy are key components of Rogue Justice Warrior courage. Gutsy behavior inspires observers, which naturally positions the Rogue Justice Warrior as a leader. Taking bold action furthers self-confidence, and boosts the Rogue Justice Warriors trust in their ability to handle any situation that presents itself.

People naturally choose to follow gutsy warriors. Indomitable Rogue Justice Warriors live by their convictions and take smart, calculated risks. Shrewd, well-timed, gambles offer a chance at huge gain. Not afraid to fail, uncompromising Rogue Justice Warriors are resilient because they face and overcome danger. Mental and emotional toughness makes it easier to withstand struggle. The gutsy Rogue Justice Warrior takes decisive steps toward ambitious goals, even when the route forward is entirely undefined.

The gritty spirit of Rogue Justice Warriors foster experimentation and the trying of new things. Openness to innovative prospects lead to breakthrough ideas and solutions. Gutsy Rogue Justice Warriors are honest, and assertive in relationships. The combination of confidence and courage leads to stronger, more authentic connections with associates. Daring Rogue Justice Warriors are not afraid to step outside their comfort zone, which opens learning and developmental opportunities.

## THE POWER OF A FIRM NO

Gutsy Rogue Justice Warriors are unabashedly strong, rigidly independent, emotionally sturdy, forceful, and dynamic. These characteristics and attributes are depicted as toxic in some circles, but your author believes that they are essential components to achieving excellence. Strength, sturdiness, and the strategic application of power expedite triumph.

Stringency in thought and deed can fluctuate somewhat from person to person, but ruggedness creates toughness. Toughness is not gender exclusive. Hard-hitting Rogue Justice Warriors will utter a firm "No" when necessary. Saying no, and having the personal discipline to not back down when challenged, are essential elements of preeminent courageousness.

## ADDITIONAL ADVANTAGES OF BEING A COURAGEOUS ROGUE JUSTIVE WARRIOR

The combination of courage and unconventional thinking triggers many advantages for the Rogue Justice Warrior. RJW's serve as the tip of the spear since they routinely act independently, challenge authority, and operate outside conventional order while displaying bravery and determination. Distinguishing oneself is standard operating procedure for a Rogue Justice Warrior.

Rogue Justice Warriors tend to think and act outside the box. These creative problem solvers are not bound by traditional approaches. Palpable nerve and daring allows them to take risks that non-rogues avoid like the plague. Courageous Rogue Justice Warriors excel at assessing hazards and acting decisively. This willingness to embrace uncertainty provides opportunity for great reward, both short and long-term.

Courageous RJW's thrive in difficult situations because they are not afraid to twist or shatter paradigms to achieve their objectives. Resilience helps them navigate challenges more effectively than those who choose to play it safe. Courageous Rogue Justice

Warriors thrive in inexact and complex environments where conventional rules and strategies do not apply. Their adaptability and boldness help them excel in situations that confound and diminish their non-rogue brethren.

A courageous Rogue Justice Warrior is not constrained by the expectations of others. Intense individuality allows them to pursue their goals *on their terms,* which results in greater self-determination and independence. True to themselves and their principles, Rogue Justice Warriors execute according to their stipulations. They drive change, make lasting impacts, and experience a deep sense of self-actualization.

## **GUTSY COURAGEOUSNESS IS INSPIRATIONAL**

Executing acts of boldness sparks a ripple effect, inspiring others to embrace their own strength. Gutsy courageousness inspires others by demonstrating what is possible when someone overcomes dread, doubt, or obstruction in pursuit of betterment, or attainment of a goal.

Motivational benefits easily apparent to Rogue Justice Warrior associates include:

- *Overcoming fear*: Gives permission for others to be strengthened and encouraged
- *Instilling hope and optimism*: Inspires optimism in those feeling powerless
- *Modeling*: Serves as an example to any witness
- *Rouses intentional action*: Induces onlookers to align choices with values and dreams
- *Enhances confidence*: Encourages others to step outside their comfort zone

## **PERSONAL COURAGE - Case Studies**

The three case study scenarios that follow provide a safe opportunity to self-assess your commitment to courageous action.

As you read, I urge you to insert yourself into each scenario. Answer the questions that follow the situation as honestly as possible. After digesting all three case studies, I encourage you to analyze and assess your personal level of rogueness.

Case Study: 1 – *Youth Sports*

Your 9-year-old son (or grandson) is playing football for the first time. It is your desire that the young man have fun, enjoy the experience, develop skills, and learn important life lessons. Age and inexperience make it obvious to any observer that the boy's skill level can accurately be assessed as early developmental.

You notice that during practice sessions the team's volunteer coaches seem to be very hardcore. The coaches physically push the players to the point of near exhaustion with few breaks and no water. If a player indicates that they are injured, the coaches ridicule perceived weakness, telling the player to toughen up and get back to practice. The coaches make it clear that winning is the only goal, and that little else matters.

As a parent/grandparent, you feel as though the coach behavior is beyond your comfort zone. You notice that teammate parents/grandparents are whispering to themselves, but no-one is acting. Do you approach the coaching staff with your concerns?

Regardless of your choice about talking to the coaches, the first game on the schedule arrives. The coaching staff is clearly amped up. Loud, excitable language and behavior trying to get the players and crowd ready to rumble. Shortly after the game gets underway, one of your son/grandson's teammates takes a hard hit. He is lying on the ground, slow to get up.

The head coach charges onto the field toward the injured player. Upon arrival, the coach aggressively yells "Get up" to the player. The coach then reaches down, grabs the players jersey, and yanks him off the ground. The player is crying. The coach yells "Don't be a damn sissy, get your ass to the bench if you're not going to play." The coach shoves the kid toward the bench, and yells "Get me somebody in here who isn't a quitter."

The question, how would you respond? Would you:

A. *Keep your thoughts to yourself as the coaches know what they are doing*
B. *Immediately approach, intervene, and challenge the coach*
C. *Choose to look the other way because coach was not THAT aggressive towards your son/grandson*
D. *Discuss the situation with other parents as soon as practical*
E. *Address your concerns with the league commissioner next week*

Case Study: 2 – *Hiring Deception*

A Fortune 500 company is experiencing high turnover rates and is chronically understaffed. The Chief Executive makes it clear to the subordinate personnel who oversee recruiting and hiring that the numbers MUST improve. The hiring Director and her supervisors feel significant pressure. The staff begins to employ various unconventional methods (including reduction of qualification guidelines) to meet perceived numerical hiring mandates.

Recruiting personnel discuss pursuing employees who may not meet established hiring criteria. Poaching non-qualified employees already in companion workforces could help the hiring team reach their acquisition quotas. Below standard expectation employees would be immediately available and could be brought onboard for less money.

Recruiters are directed to implement a strategy offering lesser qualified workers an extravagant benefit package. Of particular focus is a promise that the company seeking their services offers much better health care. The hiring manager instructs you and your co-workers to go full steam ahead with the overly generous promises designed to lure potential new hires.

The problem is that you (one of the recruiters) know that the promise of fantastic health care benefits to new hires is simply not true. Four weeks prior, you were privy to an email conversation in which discussions made it clear that the company health care package was about to be substantially reduced.

The hiring manager implies that she has no knowledge that the health benefits are about to be taken away. The hiring manager is lying, and you know it! Would you:

- ***Say nothing since revealing the deception could put your employment in jeopardy***
- ***Meet with the CEO to air your distress***
- ***Write a whistleblower letter to company Board Members***
- ***Meet privately with the aggrieved new hires after they come on-board and tell them the truth***
- ***Request a meeting with the hiring manager to address your concerns***

Case Study: 3 - *Abusive Parent*

Following a very tough week at work, you decide that a family dinner out might be just the thing to help you unwind. The entire family, including your three school age children, excitedly load into the car for the outing. When you arrive at the restaurant, everyone is seated, and the server takes your order.

The stylish restaurant is very crowded. Seated at a table near you is a family of five. A young mother and her four children. The youngsters, the oldest of which appears to be about eight years old, are being loud, unruly, and out-of-control. The oldest is pounding his silverware on the table, the middle two are arguing loudly, and the youngest is throwing everything within reach onto the floor.

The young mother appears increasingly embarrassed and frustrated. Repeatedly admonishing the kids to behave does not appear to be having the desired effect. Seemingly at wits end, the mom leaves her chair and angrily approaches the two quarrelling siblings. She yells, "I said stop it" as she (in a very hostile way) grabs them both by the collar and begins shaking them violently. Both kids burst into tears, at which time the mother aggressively said, "You shut up or I'll give you something to cry about."

Just as the mother was about to return to her seat, the youngest child knocked over her juice, spilling quite a mess onto the floor. Exasperated, the mother said, "Damn you," as she reached over, pulling the child out of the highchair. The mother, holding the child by one arm, begins to whip the 3-year-old child furiously on their rear end.

How would you react?

- *Gather your family and leave the restaurant*
- *Do nothing as it is not your place to intervene in a private family affair*
- *Step in to stop the abuse and address the offending mother*
- *Ask a manager to intercede and protect the children*
- *Take a video with your cell phone and notify police*

## **COURAGE IS VITAL**

A Rogue Justice Warrior operates outside conventional boundaries, challenging systems, norms, and authority. Courage is indispensable for a Rogue Justice Warrior because their actions inherently involve risk, uncertainty, and potential consequences. Courage permits RJW's to navigate risks with suppleness and potency. Courageous audacity helps the Rogue Justice Warrior thrive in an environment of indecision. Raw, fearless, self-assurance permits the rogue warrior to remain true to themselves.

True warriors understands that their mission is not about personal gain - it is about making a difference for others. Rogue Justice Warrior's relish challenging authority, facing hazards, confronting danger, and overcoming seemingly insurmountable odds. A capable Rogue Justice Warrior is not silent or inactive in the face of injustice. A Rogue Justice Warrior pushes forward because they know that they must not only be courageous, but also display and remain courageous.

Reflect on the three case study scenarios? How courageous and gutsy are you? Do you need to augment your personal "guts" reservoir? How much rogue is the right amount of rogue? Will you stand up to those who are blocking the path of righteousness? Are you prepared to embody the spirit of a Rogue Justice Warrior?

**F-E-A-R** "Forget Everything and Run" or
"Face Everything and Rise." The choice is yours.

*Zig Ziglar*

# Chapter 4

## *OPPOSITES AND PARADOXES*

*"So much of life is a paradox. So much of life is neither one thing or the other ... it is both at the same time"*
**David Hyde Pierce**

*"The world is full of paradoxes and life is full of opposites. The art is to embrace the opposites, accommodate the paradoxes and live with a smile."*
**Sri Sri Ravi Shankar**

### MANAGEMENT OF THE ABSURD

I want to begin this chapter by acknowledging the author and the book that years ago brought enlightenment to my thinking. Dr. Richard Farson caused me to look at life from an entirely different angle when he wrote and published the book ***Management of the Absurd – Paradoxes in Leadership*** in 1996. I highly recommend that you add this title to your reading list. When you move toward the concepts in Dr. Farson's book, it can literally change the way that you look at world paradigms.

Dr. Farson's book is focused on management and leadership practices. However, once you comprehend and adopt the hypothesis of Dr. Farson's philosophies, you will see that his unique perspective leads you to process your thoughts differently. The concepts revealed in ***Management of the Absurd*** seem contradictory and confusing at first blush, however, serious contemplation reveals their brilliance. Much of the composition that follows in this chapter has been inspired by Dr. Farson and his work. Salute!

## **OPPOSITES, PARADOXES, AND ROGUE JUSTICE**

You may be thinking; what in the world do opposites and paradoxes have to do with the theme of this book? Everything, things are not always as they seem. The answer encompasses the very premise of **Rogue Justice**. The essence of this book is understanding that every issue has multiple, often opposing, perspectives. Rarely, if ever, is there only one viable solution to any problem, challenge, conundrum, dilemma, predicament, or quandary. True wisdom, the secret sauce, lies in our ability to challenge conformist thinking and remain open to alternative interpretations.

Idioms such as "There is more than one way to skin a cat," "Spill the beans," and "Different strokes for different folks" make it clear that words and phrases can mean something entirely different from the literal meaning of the verse. The terms rogue and rogue justice exemplify this duality. In other words, they have one meaning when the syntax is considered negatively, but, the identical word(s), when viewed on the other side of the same coin, can represent the opposite perspective.

Think back to Chapter 1 when we discussed the traditional definition of what it means to be rogue. Conventional thinking tells us that rogues and rogue behavior should be viewed negatively since the term(s) have been used to depict a form of homo sapien rascal for hundreds of years. Unreliable, treacherous, unmanageable, and disorderly scoundrels they said, whose illicit and unlawful behavior is frequently disgraceful.

However, **Rogue Justice** makes a very strong case that rogues, particularly honorable rogues fighting for justice (Rogue Justice Warriors), can be, and should be, viewed through a positive optical prism. Since reputable, high-performing rogues are the practitioners of Rogue Justice Warrior behavior, it is well-defined that their qualities and conduct lead to the pinnacle of desirable outcome. Upon completion of this book, undeniable evidence will illuminate that a Rogue Justice Warrior is literally the exact opposite of the rogue miscreant described throughout history.

The paragraphs that follow expound on my rogue supposition in greater detail.

## **APPRECIATING OPPOSITES**

Hippocrates, Socrates, Aristotle, Galen, and many other noted scholars discussed the concept of opposites (Latin; unio oppositorum) many centuries ago. No doubt there is much collective intellectual learning attributed to the study of opposites. For the purposes of **Rogue Justice,** I propose that we focus upon modest, clear-cut, uncomplicated truisms easily applicable and understood.

The Cambridge dictionary defines opposite (noun), as "Something or someone that is completely different from another person or thing." Every material has an opposite; undeniably, we live in a world of opposites. Objects or matters can be diametrically different, yet dependent upon each other. Opposites are frequently interconnected, and opposite things can be simultaneously true.

It seems obvious that few things are as closely related as opposites. Opposites authenticate one another. Their harmony is that one exists because the opposite is necessary for the existence of the other. Paradoxically, when we look closely, we can often see that there is a singleness to things initially believed to be dissimilar. Opposites are utterly contradictory, yet contingent upon each other for coexistence.

Common, everyday examples of opposite properties include:

- Positive           Negative
- Ugliness           Beauty
- Hot                Cold
- Accurate           Inaccurate
- Dying              Living
- Upward             Downward

- Good     Bad
- True     False
- Light     Dark
- Timid     Bold
- Clean     Dirty
- Innocent     Guilty
- Wise     Unwise
- Defeat     Victory
- Absent     Present
- Awake     Asleep
- Daytime     Nighttime

Misfit rogue qualities and behavior are contradictory to those exhibited by Rogue Justice Warriors. The following depicts the contrasts between scandalous rogues and a desirable Rogue Justice Warrior.

| **Rogue** | **Rogue Justice Warrior** |
| --- | --- |
| Scoundrel | Protagonist Hero |
| Questionable Mores | Righteous |
| Illegitimate | Authentic |
| Dastardly | Gallant |
| Foolish | Astute |
| Tricksters | Straight Shooter |
| Fraudulent Chicanery | Honorable |
| Egocentric | Altruistic |
| Uncontrollable Degenerate | Upstanding |

## **REAL WORLD PARADOXICAL SITUATIONS**

*Case Study # 1 – Athletic Dominance*

    A 11-year-old athlete has been playing baseball for three years. His natural athletic capability is well above that of his peers. Whether running the bases, or attempting to steal a base, he is by far the fastest runner on his travel team. While hitting, this young fellow has tremendous power that exceeds that of his contemporaries. He hits home runs over the fence consistently. The young athlete also possesses the strongest arm on the team, throwing with much more pace and distance than any teammate.

At a young age, our young superstar athlete is enormously effective on the field. However, coaches experience tremendous frustration with the prodigy because he has a bad attitude. He is not a good teammate. Smart-mouthed, negative, and condescending to fellow players, he is resistant to drills and workouts, viewing them as unnecessary and as a waste of time.

Fast forward thru his baseball career. Each season, the superstar's athletic advantage becomes less because he fails to continuously develop himself. Peer players, who continue to work and expand their skillsets, begin to equal, and/or surpass the superstar in performance. By the time that the prodigy is a senior in high school, he is a very average performer.

The paradox in this situation is that the prodigy's superior natural ability at a young age effectively hindered his development. Because it was so easy for him to excel with minimal effort as a youngster, he never developed the mindset, nor the work ethic needed for continued top-quality improvement. Sluggish self-growth and overreliance on biological talent led to eventual mediocrity.

*Case Study # 2 – Shit Sandwich*

Sad to say, but most who have worked for a boss have experienced or witnessed the shit sandwich technique. Used by low competent or toxic bosses, the shit sandwich is too often thought to be a feedback tool. The process involves giving workers negative feedback sandwiched neatly between two positive points.

The idea behind the shit sandwich approach to furnishing criticism is a belief that negative feedback is easier for personnel to tolerate if it is preceded, and followed, by positive reinforcement. The wrongdoing boss will lamely impart a compliment which is intended to please the recipient, lesson tension, and pave the way for the nastiness about to follow. The second element of a shit sandwich is the negative or critical comments. After dropping the nasty bomb on the recipient, the donor attempts to ease the pain of the detonation by adding another compliment.

Many do not like the inauthentic nature of a feeble compliment. Studies show that most employees do not respond well to negative feedback (Green, Paul, Harvard Business School). And, sometimes those who experience the shit sandwich phenomenon come away feeling that they were doing well because they focus only on the two positive comments.

The paradox of the shit sandwich technique is that the result of the procedure is completely at odds with the intent of the stratagem. The shit sandwich does not please the palate of the recipient. The most common result is a foul aftertaste left in the employee's mouth.

*Case Study # 3 – Iatrogenic Mishaps*

The Hippocratic Oath, named for Hippocrates, the father of medicine, famously instructs Doctors to "First, do no harm." The intent of this directive to physicians implies that medical professionals have an obligation to follow regimens that they consider beneficial to their patients. The pledge encourages medical practitioners to give priority to the avoidance of damage.

Ironically, the best intentions and efforts of medical professionals often backfire. The term iatrogenic means words or actions induced unintentionally in a patient by a physician. Literally, the opposite of what was intended. In layman's terms, iatrogenic mishaps refer to new injuries or medical complications resulting from treatment. Common examples include complications from surgery, side effects from drugs, and hospital infections.

The paradox of iatrogenic mishaps is that sometimes the result of treatment is worse than the disease. Unintentional as it may be, often the result of heroic efforts to positively impact a medicinal issue turns into a violation of the Hippocratic Oath. Efforts to do good can easily create the reverse of the envisioned outcome.

## SUMMARY

Even though the content of this chapter may have seemed completely left field when you first saw it, I hope that readers now understand how the world of opposites and paradoxes intersect with **Rogue Justice**. The definition of a rogue (and rogue behavior) does not manifest with one-size fits all rogue criterion. I encourage readers to embrace paradoxical thinking. Be open to the possibility that there can always be more than meets the eye. What seems readily apparent on first blush, may only scratch the surface of true insight.

Rogue Justice Warriors know that marvelous solutions come in various shapes and sizes. They break new ground, using innovative, novel strategies and solutions that enable excellence. One with a knack for knowledge can reconcile opposing things. To appreciate one side, you must know the other. So, it is with **Rogue Justice**. It is our job as Rogue Justice Warriors to take a fresh look. Recognition of opposites and paradoxes allows us to see beyond surface-level truths and unlock deeper insights.

*"If you can't solve a problem, it is because you are playing by the rules"*

**Paul Arden**

# Chapter 5

## *JUSTICE*

*"Every time that we turn our heads the other way when we see the law flouted, when we tolerate what we know to be wrong, when we close our eyes and ears to the corrupt because we are too busy or too frightened, when we fail to speak up and speak out, we strike a blow against freedom, decency, and justice"*

**Robert Kennedy**

Justice is a concept that seems simple and self-evident. However, as we shall see throughout this chapter, the concept of justice is multi-faceted and quite complex. Our study will reveal that justice may simultaneously represent fragments of lawfulness, fairness, parity, equity, evenhandedness, uprightness, impartiality, justness, rightfulness, legitimateness, and morality.

Derived from the Latin *jus* (right or law), justice is often equated with fairness. The Oxford English Dictionary defines the "just" person as one who typically "Does what is morally right." The *Institutes of Justinian*, a sixth-century codification of Roman law, features the "Constant and perpetual will to render to each his due." Fairness, often seen as a synonym of justice, helps us to understand how proportional distribution is related to equitable dissemination.

It is quite easy to see that the absence of justice, or injustice, is a fundamental quality of life issue. This is why righteousness, integrity, and self-determination are key to our hypothesis regarding ***Rogue Justice***. Going rogue without a noble cause is hollow, lacking, and non-virtuous. Without justice as a motive, I suspect that rogues would too often resemble the scoundrels described in Chapter 1. As we shall see going forward, the level of individual rogueness is frequently tied directly to excellence, equality, and merited results. Renowned philosopher Lao Tzu taught that "Highly evolved people have their own conscience as pure law."

The sections that follow will help the reader explore various forms of law, integrity, and equity. Lastly, this chapter will analyze the intersection of justice, rogue justice, and Rogue Justice Warriors. As you shall discover, the three are irrefutably interrelated.

## **THE MANY FACES OF JUSTICE**

*Religious Justice:* Rooted in divine authority, this view asserts that justice originates from God. Advocates of Divine Command theory say justice, and indeed the whole of morality, is the authoritative command of God. Some versions assert that God must be obeyed because of the nature of God's relationship with humanity. Jews, Christians, and Muslims traditionally believe that justice is derived from and held by God (**Wikipedia.org**).

*Due Process - Legal Justice:* Ensures fairness through laws, courts, and enforcement mechanisms. It relies on the impartial application of statutes and regulations. (legaldictionary.io) Governments pursue legal justice by operating courts and enforcing their rulings. (**legaldictionary.io**).

*Retributive Justice:* Focuses on the punishment of lawbreakers and the compensation of victims. In general, the severity of the punishment should be proportionate to the seriousness of the crime (**Britannica.com**).

*Reparative Justice:* Centers on repairing past harms and preventing future injustices, often through financial compensation. (nebhe.org/reparative-justice).

*Distributive Justice* concerns the fair allocation of resources among diverse members of a community. The principle implies that every person should have approximately the same level of material goods and services. Distributive justice focuses on equal social and economic outcomes (thoughtco.com).

## **TRIAL BY JURY**

Trial by a jury of one's peers is often held up as the preeminent path to justice. While true that contemporaneous evaluation of applicable facts does offer potential protections against bias, inaccurate verdicts still happen. Recent research suggests that up to 4% of individuals receive an incorrect verdict, judgment, or penalty as an outcome of a jury trial (Gaille, Louise, 2020).

Trial evaluation as a justice benchmark can be problematic since statistically, trials are rare. About 94 percent of felony convictions at the state level and about 97 percent at the federal level are the result of plea bargains (themarshallproject.com).

Plea bargains involve a pre-trial deal between prosecutors and defense attorneys. These are agreements struck between the government triers of fact and the accused in which the defendant admits guilt and gives up their right to a formal trial in exchange for favorable sentencing terms. Plea bargains allow courts to clear cases faster and avoid trial costs. There is much debate as to the effect of plea bargain transactions upon the actual attainment of justice.

## **CASE STUDIES**

*Justice Case Study #1 -Tiananmen Square Tank Challengers Facing down the Chinese army*

In 1989, student-led protests and demonstrations called for democratic reform in China. Tens of thousands of protesters marched from Beijing to Tiananmen Square. The reformers, facing lack of jobs and increasing poverty, wanted improvements to the educational system. Many initiated hunger strikes to make their point.

As the movement grew, the Chinese government became increasingly uncomfortable with the protests. The government instituted martial law, which significantly eliminated many student rights. 250,000 government troops were dispatched to Tiananmen Square to quell the civil disturbance. In response to the government crackdown, student protestor ranks grew to more than a million people.

Daily marches and vigils increased the agitation level of the authorities. On June 4, 1989, Chinese soldiers and police stormed Tiananmen Square, firing live rounds into the crowd. Many protestors simply tried to escape, but others fought back, stoning the attacking troops, and setting fire to military vehicles. Reporters and western diplomats in Beijing that day estimated that hundreds to thousands of protesters were killed in the Tiananmen Square Massacre, and as many as 10,000 were arrested. Worldwide condemnation of the Chinese government followed the massacre.

The image of an unidentified man standing alone in defiance and blocking a column of Chinese tanks serves as an iconic reminder of the events in Tiananmen Square. The unidentified Rogue Justice Warrior fighting for his cause will be forever known as the Tiananmen Square Tank Man.

*Sources*: USAToday.com, BBC.com and CNN.com

## *Justice Case Study # 2 - American Gymnast Stripped of Bronze Medal*

In one of the most controversial incidents in Olympic history, American gymnast Jordan Chiles was stripped of the bronze medal that she won for floor exercise in Paris. Following a scoring controversy, the International Olympic Committee ordered the 23-year-old American to return her medal after a court ruled it had been awarded to her improperly.

Upon completion of her floor exercise during the competition, Chiles was in fourth position. Her coach submitted what is known as an inquiry about her score. Following a successful challenge, Chiles' score was increased, which caused her to leapfrog the closest competitor and capture the bronze medal. The Court of Arbitration for Sport (CAS), and the International Olympic Committee (IOC) subsequently found that the scoring inquiry by the U.S. coach was invalid. The committees relied upon procedural technicalities, saying that the coach made the initial verbal appeal *four seconds too late*, thus causing it to be unacceptable.

USA Gymnastics pushed back, submitting an appeal of the CAS ruling including a letter and video evidence that it said proved the inquiry of Chiles' score was filed within the one-minute deadline. The U.S. also alleged that they were not given adequate time or notice to effectively challenge the decision. Furthermore, the U.S. alleged that they were disputing significant procedural errors, and questioned the impartiality of the panel that decided the Chiles case since the President of the deciding panel had represented Romanian athletes in other cases.

The Court of Arbitration for Sport (CAS) declared that their rules did not allow for an arbitral award to be reconsidered even when conclusive new evidence is presented. USA Gymnastics said in a statement that Chiles was denied a meaningful opportunity to be heard. "We are deeply disappointed by the notification and will continue to pursue every possible avenue and appeal process," they said.

Chiles and the U.S. Olympic Committee have indicated that the pursuit of truth and justice in the matter remains unwavering. Jordan Chiles has said "I have no words. This decision feels unjust and comes as a significant blow. I will never waver from my values of competing with integrity, striving for excellence, upholding the values of sportsmanship and the rules that dictate fairness. I am now confronted with one of the most challenging moments of my career. I will approach this challenge as I have the others - and will make every effort to ensure that justice is done" said Rogue Justice Warrior athlete Jordan Chiles.

*Sources*: USAToday.com NBC.com and Today.com

*Justice Case Study # 3 - Due Process*

The core facts in the William's case are as follows; A prosecutor had significant personal involvement in a death penalty case during his tenure as District Attorney of Philadelphia. The defendant, following conviction and appeal, alleged that the prosecutor's office had engaged in prosecutorial misconduct during the investigation of his case and his trial.

After a post-conviction court agreed with the defendant, the state appealed, sending the case to the Pennsylvania Supreme Court. Problem was, the prosecutor who had handled the case in district court was now the Chief Justice of the State Supreme Court. The Chief Justice refused to recuse himself from the case, finding that his office had not engaged in misconduct. The Chief Justice publicly chastised the Williams defense attorneys in the process.

The U.S. Supreme Court found that the failure of the Chief State Justice to recuse himself from a case in which he was previously involved violated an individual's rights under the Constitution. The Supreme Court recognized the clear conflict of interest in this case, recognizing that impartial adjudicators are essential to ensuring due process. Due process of law was upheld under the 14$^{th}$ amendment theory that all must have access to impartial, equal, exact justice. In this case, the Pennsylvania Supreme Court justices became the Rogue Justice Warriors who insured that lawfulness was done.

*Source*: Williams v. Pennsylvania: A True Case of Judicial Bias, Fordant, Christina

## *Justice Case Study Case # 4 - Public Water Crisis*

The city of Flint, Michigan was embroiled in a multi-year financial crisis. The City Manager was feeling pressure to save money at any cost. The effort to reduce costs led to a decision regarding switching the city's water supply from Lake Huron to the Flint River. I think it fair to say that the city did not adequately consider the potential risk to public health.

Residents and leaders were aware of the history of the Flint River. Even though the Flint River had caught fire twice in the past, it was estimated that treatment for the new water supply would reasonably cost between $80-100.00 per day. Unfortunately, the pump to facilitate the chemical treatment was never installed. Flint, Michigan found itself experiencing a full-blown toxic public water crisis,

The water disaster in Flint prevented the safe drinking of public water. Bacteria caused residents problems with bathing and showering. Damaged lead pipes facilitated structural emergency exposure problems that took years to correct. Dr. Mona Hanna-Allisha, a crusading pediatrician, and author of **What the Eyes Don't See**, brought the fight for justice in Flint to the national spotlight.

Dr. Allisha's personal advocacy used science to prove that Flint residents (especially children) were dangerously exposed to lead. She courageously went public with her research and faced a brutal backlash. With persistence and single-minded sense of mission, she spoke truth to power. She shone a light on how misguided austerity policies and callous bureaucratic indifference placed an entire city at risk. Dr. Mona Hanna-Allisha proved to be a Rogue Justice Warrior who made sure that social justice activism helped turn the Flint crisis around.

*Sources*: *"Pediatrician Who Exposed Flint Water Crisis Shares Her Story of Resistance,"* June 25, 2018, Terry Gross. https://monahannaattisha.com

## **NO JUSTICE**

Appeasement, leniency, and ineffective action enable injustice. History has shown time and again that pacification frequently leads to greater noncompliance. The soft, no hammer, acquiesce approach to a dispute has no teeth, and as such will surely undermine conformity and/or change. Neville Chamberlin's failed attempt to pacify Adolf Hitler at the beginning of WW 2 is but one glaring case study that supports these points unequivocally.

Meekness, docile conduct, and temperate positions frequently impede the administration of justice. Weak, soft mindsets and techniques keep us from successfully solving problems and attaining goals. One who rolls over and plays dead will be feckless, leading to disappointment and malfunction. Failure to use the backbone when appropriate practically guarantees that the battle is unwinnable.

When faced with tough, high-risk dilemmas, we have the freedom to select our response. One must actively confront injustice rather than surrender to it. Rogue Justice Warriors choose to confront, not to act like losers!

## **WHY *ROGUE* JUSTICE?**

As discussed throughout this chapter, justice can be an elusive target. Uncontaminated equality is the bedrock of a sophisticated society. Impartiality, objectivity, neutrality, and evenhandedness in the application of law are principles that civilized societies aspire to attain. To the extent possible, all people should be treated the same way. Consistent application of standards, mores, and regulations help ensure that righteousness reigns as the rule of the day.

As demonstrated by the case studies earlier in this section, even in the most exceptional cultures, injustice rears its ugly head far too often. Occasionally, unfairness occurs without malice. Sometimes, wrongness is the result of deliberate nastiness. Frequently the nauseating inequality culprit is corruption. Regardless the source of the injustice, overturning an unfair outcome requires

# ROGUE JUSTICE

deliberate and compelling intervention. Rogue Justice Warriors understand that sitting on their hands hoping that change will occur innately, is not a successful nullification strategy.

Rogue Justice Warriors use whatever tools necessary to ensure that the right thing comes to pass. Rogue Justice Warriors go outside established boundaries to ensure equitable outcomes. Purposeful intercession, irregular tactics, and approaches independent of norms are in play when an illicit outcome needs to be overturned. All ethical options should be on the table. Rectifying a wrong, and doing the right thing, often requires working beyond established parameters to get the job done.

Rogue Justice Warriors are the practitioners of **Rogue Justice**. Rogue Justice Warriors use their phenomenal skills for good. They willingly join the fight for parity because quashing wrongs, abolishing inequity, or invalidating injustice is simply what they do. A Rogue Justice Warrior nobly and rebelliously performs according to their robust personal code of conscience. They are patriots, who do arduous things when they need to be accomplished. Because they stand up to disgraceful abuses, Rogue Justice Warriors are cultural heroes, societal guardians of just outcomes!

Without Rogue Justice Warrior intervention, true justice is routinely absent. Do not let injustice occur on your watch. Step up, roar like a lion, and fight like a honey badger. When the opportunity to be a Rogue Justice Warrior presents itself (and it will habitually), seize the moment, annihilate the injustice, be significant, and be proud! You can be the difference maker!

# Chapter 6

## *HISTORIC ROGUE PROTAGONISTS*

### WHAT IS A PROTAGONIST?

To fully appreciate the potency of rogue behavior—its respectability, righteousness, compelling nature, and capacity to achieve extraordinary accomplishments—we turn to Dictionary.com for clarity. According to this source, a protagonist is defined in three primary ways:

1. The leading character, hero, or heroine in a theatrical drama or other literary work.
2. A proponent or advocate of a political cause, social program, etc.
3. The leader or principal figure in a movement or cause.

### HERO, ADVOCATE FOR A CAUSE, LEADER OF A MOVEMENT

The term protagonist is derived from ancient Greek, meaning "first struggler" or "one who struggles against" (Merriam-Webster.com). Struggle, conflict, and perseverance are frequently the essence of a protagonist's journey. The protagonist, or hero, is commonly involved in skirmishes of some kind, either against a rival, perilous circumstances, or possibly in furtherance of their convictions.

You will recall the traits, characteristics, and actions personified by a Rogue Justice Warrior as discussed in Chapter 1. It is precisely these attributes and behaviors that differentiate the high performing rogue from an undesirable troublemaker. Noble rogue protagonists, or Rogue Justice Warriors, are easy to identify, unmistakably unmatched among peers. Exceptional performers, these heroes embody and facilitate greatness.

People who shape history, powerhouse individuals, larger than life doers, have made the world what it is from ancient times until modern day. These extraordinary influencers share many common beliefs and behaviors. Significantly, Rogue Justice Warriors all have a willingness to challenge the status quo. By and large, they are rebels, willing to take on established norms and traditions because of exceptionally robust private philosophies.

The following seven (7) mega VIPs are but a few of the many throughout time who exemplify the essence of a Rogue Justice Warrior. As you explore their remarkable story summaries, I encourage you to recognize, analyze, and appreciate the roguish elements of their modus operandi.

# JESUS CHRIST

Most scholars agree that Jesus was likely born around 4 – 6 BC in Bethlehem, about six miles from Jerusalem. His parents, Joseph, and Mary, took him to Egypt to avoid a massacre of infant boys ordered by King Herod. The family returned to their home in Nazareth in what is now northern Israel after King Herod's death. (www.Christianity.org).

*Christ is – Artistic representation of Jesus, c.1130. Andreas Wahra*

During his lifetime, Jesus' teachings were radical, counter-cultural, and revolutionary. He inspired and challenged the people who heard him, but antagonized most of the Jewish religious leaders. The Pharisees were upset by Jesus' doctrine and apparent breach of laws regarding the Jewish Sabbath. They began openly challenging and mocking Jesus. Religious authorities eventually conspired with one of Jesus' closest followers (Judas Iscariot) to have him arrested for blasphemy.

## **Biblical Accounts of Jesus' Mindset and Behavior**

Many Bible stories highlight the mindset and conduct of Jesus. The accounts that follow are but a few examples of Rogue Justice Warrior behavior by a man that many believe to be a prophet and Christian guardian angel.

*Jesus Teaching Lessons on the Sabbath*

Excerpt from **Matthew 12:8 (KJV)**

Or have ye not read in the law, how that on the sabbath days the priests in the temple profane the sabbath, and are blameless? But I say unto you, that in this place is one greater than the temple. For the son of man is Lord even of the sabbath day.

Excerpt from **Luke 6:1-11 Bible.com (NIV)**

On another sabbath, he entered the synagogue and taught, and there was a man there whose right hand was withered. The scribes and the Pharisees watched him to see whether he would cure on the sabbath, so that they might find an accusation against him. Even though he knew what they were thinking, he said to the man who had the withered hand, "Come and stand here." He got up and stood there. Then Jesus said to them, "I ask you, is it lawful to do good or to do harm on the sabbath, to save life or to destroy it?" After looking around at all of them, he said to him, "Stretch out your hand." He did so, and his hand was restored. But they [Pharisees] were filled with fury and discussed with one another what they might do to Jesus.

Jesus' defiance enraged religious leaders, fueling their desire to eliminate him.

*Jesus and the Woman of Samaria*

Excerpt from: **John 4:1-42 (NIV)**

So, he came to a town in Samaria called Sychar, near the plot of ground Jacob had given to his son Joseph. Jacob's well was there, and Jesus, tired as he was from the journey, sat down by the well. It was about noon.

When a Samaritan woman came to draw water, Jesus said to her, "Will you give me a drink?" The Samaritan woman said to him, "You are a Jew and I am a Samaritan woman. How can you ask me for a drink?" Jesus answered her, "If you knew the gift of God and who it is that asks you for a drink, you would have asked him and he would have given you living water."

"Sir," the woman said, "you have nothing to draw with and the well is deep. Where can you get this living water? Are you greater than our father Jacob, who gave us the well and drank from it himself, as did also his sons and his livestock?"

Jesus answered, "Everyone who drinks this water will be thirsty again, but whoever drinks the water I give them will never thirst. Indeed, the water I give them will become in them a spring of water welling up to eternal life."

The woman said to him, "Sir, give me this water so that I won't get thirsty and have to keep coming here to draw water." He told her, "Go, call your husband and come back." "I have no husband," she replied. Jesus said to her, "You are right when you say you have no husband. The fact is, you have had five husbands, and the man you now have is not your husband. What you have just said is quite true."

"Sir," the woman said, "I can see that you are a prophet. "Woman," Jesus replied, "believe me, a time is coming when you will worship the Father neither on this mountain nor in Jerusalem. God is spirit, and his worshipers must worship in the Spirit and in truth." The woman said, "I know that Messiah" is coming. When he comes, he will explain everything to us." Then Jesus declared, "I, the one speaking to you-I am he."

Just then his disciples returned and were surprised to find him talking with a woman. But no one asked, "What do you want?" or "Why are you talking with her?" Then, leaving her water jar, the woman went back to the town and said to the people, "Come, see a man who told me everything I ever did. Could this be the Messiah?" They came out of the town and made their way toward him.

This story demonstrates that Jesus openly engaged with a Samaritan woman, defying gender, and ethnic divisions of the time. He offered her "living water" symbolizing eternal salvation. And his act of inclusion and compassion challenged societal prejudices and reshaped religious outreach.

This bold act cemented Jesus' role as a disruptor of corruption and injustice.

*Jesus Cleanses the Temple*

Excerpt from **John 2:13–17 (NKJV)**

Now the Passover of the Jews was at hand, and Jesus went up to Jerusalem. He found in the temple those who sold oxen and sheep and doves, and the money changers doing business.

He had made a whip of cords, He drove them all out of the temple, with the sheep and the oxen, and poured out the changers' money and overturned the tables. And he said to those who sold doves, "Take these things away!" and "Do not make my father's house a house of merchandise!" Then His disciples remembered that it was written, "Zeal for your house has eaten me up."

**Biblical Account of Jesus' Death**

In about 30 ADS, Jesus was arrested. He went before Jewish and Roman authorities charged with blasphemy. The Pharisees and the crowd demanded the death penalty. (www.Christianity.org.uk).

*Crucifixion*

Excerpt from **Luke 23:26-49 (New International Version)**

Two others, who were criminals, were led away to be put to death with him. And when they came to the place that is called the skull, there they crucified him, and the criminals, one on his right and one on his left. And Jesus said, "Father, forgive them, for they know not what they do." And they cast lots to divide his garments. And the people stood by, watching, but the rulers scoffed at him, saying, "He saved others; let him save himself, if he is the Christ of God, his Chosen One!"

The soldiers mocked him, coming up and offering him sour wine and saying, if you are the King of the Jews, save yourself, they said. There was also an inscription over him, "This is the King of the Jews." One of the criminals who were hanged railed at him, saying, "Are you not the Christ? Save yourself and us!" But the other rebuked him, saying, "Do you not fear God, since you are under the same sentence of condemnation?

And we indeed justly accused, for we are receiving the due reward of our deeds; but this man has done nothing wrong." And he said, "Jesus, remember me when you come into your kingdom." And he said to him, "Truly, I say to you, today you will be with me in Paradise."

It was now about the sixth hour, and there was darkness over the whole land until the ninth hour, while the sun's light failed. And the curtain of the temple was torn in two. Then Jesus, calling out with a loud voice, said, "Father, into your hands I commit my spirit!" And having said this he breathed his last. Now when the centurion saw what had taken place, he praised God, saying, "Certainly this man was innocent!" And all the crowd that had assembled for this spectacle, when they saw what had taken place, returned home beating their breasts. And all his acquaintances and the women who had followed him from Galilee stood at a distance watching these things.

### ❖ *Confirmed Rogue Justice Warrior*

Jesus of Nazareth, considered by many to be the Messiah of the Christian faith, was highly controversial, yet insanely impactful.

# HARRIET TUBMAN

Harriet Tubman was born a slave c. 1820, in Dorchester County, Maryland. Her given name was Araminta Ross. Early in her life, she adopted her mother's first name of Harriet. In 1849, she fled to Philadelphia, Pennsylvania because she had heard talk that she was about to be sold. While escaping slavery, she left behind a husband, siblings, and her parents. Harriet Tubman went on to become a leading abolitionist before the American Civil War.

Over the course of her life, Harriet Tubman served as a nurse, a union spy, and a woman suffrage supporter. However, she is most famously known as a "Conductor" of the Underground Railroad. The Underground Railroad was a complex network of secret safe houses that helped enslaved people seek freedom to the North.

### **Rogue Courage and Fortitude Exhibited Early in Life**

At about age five, Harriet was hired out to work, initially serving as a nursemaid and later as a field hand, a cook, and a woodcutter. (Johnston, Brittanica.com). As a nursemaid, she was whipped when one of her babies cried, leaving her with permanent emotional and physical scars (history.com).

Around the age of 12, Harriet's craving for justice manifested itself. She spotted an overseer about to punish a slave by throwing a heavy weight at the alleged fugitive. Harriet stepped between the enslaved person and the boss. The heavy weight struck Tubman in the head. The weight broke her skull, leaving her with seizures, headaches, hallucinations, and narcolepsy for the rest of her life. (history.com).

## Work in the Underground Railroad

With the help of the Underground Railroad, Harriet escaped to freedom in 1849. Her first journey leading others occurred in December 1850, when she led her niece and two children to freedom. That excursion was the first of 13 progressively more dangerous trips over the next decade. It is believed that she led at least 70 run-away slaves thru the Underground Railroad to Canada. Some reports credit her with saving as many as 300 people, though precise numbers are impossible to verify.

If an escapee endangered the mission by attempting to abandon the journey and return home, Harriet Tubman reportedly threatened them with a gun, saying "You'll be free or die." (history.com). Her reputation as an innovator was cemented when she began leading escape missions on Saturday nights. Sunday was a day of rest, so a Saturday night escape increased the odds of success since the getaways would not be reported in newspapers until Monday.

The most famous conductor in the Underground Railroad, Mrs. Tubman became known as the "Moses of her people." It has been said that she never lost a fugitive she was leading to freedom (www.Harriet-Tubman.org). Rewards were offered by slaveholders for Tubman's capture, while abolitionists celebrated her courage. From 1862 to 1865 she served as a scout, a spy, nurse, and laundress, for Union forces (www.Harriet-Tubman.org).

## After the Civil War

Following the Civil War, Tubman returned to life on her small farm in Auburn, New York. She showed particular concern for orphans and older black adults. Through the generosity of donors such as AME Zion Church, and a local bank, she was able to acquire land thru an auction. Eventually, the Harriet Tubman Home for Aged and Indigent Negroes became a reality. Harriet Tubman herself became a patient at the home from 1911 until her death in 1913 (www.nps.gov).

In 2024, the United States government authorized the U.S. Mint to issue $5 gold coins, $1 silver coins, and half dollar clad coins to recognize the bicentennial of Harriet Tubman's birth (www.usmint.gov).

❖ ***Confirmed Rogue Justice Warrior***

Harriet Tubman, considered by many to be one of the most courageous and groundbreaking women in American history, was highly controversial, yet insanely impactful.

# GENERAL GEORGE PATTON

General George S. Patton, nicknamed "Old blood and guts," commanded the Seventh United States Army in the Mediterranean theater of World War II, and the Third United States Army in France and Germany following the Allied invasion of Normandy in June 1944 (militaryhistorynow.com). His larger-than-life presence, strict discipline, and motivational speeches inspired his troops and left a lasting impression on both his contemporaries and history.

Patton cultivated a reputation as a maverick, a radical reformer. He was outspoken, unconventional, and defiant. However, his speeches and actions were inspirational to the troops. Patton was known for brusque, controversial statements, but he was also notorious for his aggressive and bold military tactics. General Patton advocated for armored warfare and is recognized as playing a significant role in developing U.S. Army tank tactics and strategy (militaryhistorynow.com)

www.ecrater.com

## Awards and Commendations

General George Patton was one of the most highly decorated officers in United States military history. His military recognition and honors include:

**Distinguished Service Cross** (2 Awards): Awarded for extraordinary heroism in action against an enemy.

**Distinguished Service Medal** (3 Awards): Recognized exceptional meritorious service to the government in a duty of great responsibility.

**Silver Star** (2 Awards): Awarded for gallantry in action against an enemy.

**Legion of Merit**: Awarded for exceptionally meritorious conduct in the performance of outstanding services and achievements.

**Bronze Star Medal**: Recognized acts of heroism, acts of merit, or meritorious service in a combat zone.

**Purple Heart**: Awarded for being wounded or killed in any action against an enemy of the United States.

**Air Medal**: Awarded for single acts of heroism or meritorious achievement while participating in aerial flight.

**Mexican Border Service Medal**: Recognized service during the Pancho Villa Expedition.

**World War I Victory Medal**: Awarded for service during World War I.

**American Defense Service Medal**: Recognized military service during the limited emergency period before the United States' entry into World War II.

**European-African-Middle Eastern Campaign Medal with Bronze Arrowhead**

**World War II Victory Medal**: Awarded for service during World War II.

**Army of Occupation Medal**: Recognized service in the occupation of Germany following World War II.

    In addition to his American honors, General Patton also received the following foreign decorations:

**Order of the Bath (United Kingdom)**: An honorary knighthood recognizing distinguished service.

**Order of the British Empire (United Kingdom)**: Recognized meritorious service to the British Empire.

**Croix de Guerre (France and Belgium)**: Awarded for acts of heroism in combat with the enemy.

**Legion of Honor (France)**: Recognized extraordinary military or civilian merit.

**Order of the White Lion** (Czechoslovakia): Awarded for exceptional services to Czechoslovakia.

**Order of Ouissam Alaouite** (Morocco): Recognized distinguished services to Morocco. Source: (pattonhq.com, Province, 2024)

## **Controversies and Challenges**

In 1943, during the Sicily Campaign, General Patton was involved in two separate incidents where he slapped and derogatorily denounced soldiers who were being treated for battle fatigue (PTSD). He accused them of cowardice, and slapped them in front of medical personnel and other soldiers. These incidents led to public outrage, a reprimand from General Eisenhower, and Patton's temporary removal from command.

Near the end of World War II and shortly afterward, Patton made repeated controversial remarks about the Soviet Union, suggesting that the U.S. should be prepared to confront the Soviets militarily following WW II. His outspoken anti-Soviet views were at odds with the official government policy of the time that focused upon cooperation with the Soviet Union.

Near the end of the war, Patton made public statements regarding former Nazis, suggesting that not all Nazis were bad and criticizing the denazification process. He believed that former Nazis were necessary for the administration and rebuilding of Germany. At the time, using Nazi's to move forward was highly controversial.

Patton's public outspokenness led to significant criticism from both military and political leaders. General Eisenhower removed Patton's command, assigning him to the Fifteenth Army. The significantly less prestigious post effectively sidelined him from further noteworthy military operations.

Patton's diary and some of his public statements revealed racist and anti-Semitic views, which were controversial both during his time, and in historical assessments of his character and legacy.

### End of General George Patton

On December 9, 1945, Patton was sitting in the back of a limousine when his driver sped over a railroad crossing in Manheim, Germany, and plowed into the passenger-side of a left-turning Army truck headed into a depot. A head injury caused the general to be rushed to a hospital in Heidelberg. A blood clot worked its way to his heart. At 5:55 p.m. on December 21, 1945, General George passed away in his sleep, ending the life of one of America's greatest battlefield commanders. All of Patton's military laurels could not protect him from a simple car accident that occurred only eight months after WW II ended. (nationalww11museum.org).

❖ *<u>Confirmed Rogue Justice Warrior</u>*

General George Patton, considered by many to be America's most effective military Commander of all time, was highly controversial, yet insanely impactful.

# TASUNKE WITKO (CRAZY HORSE)

Crazy Horse, or Tasunke Witko, was born around 1840 in what is now South Dakota. At the time, the Lakota Nation was seeking to expand their territory into the Trans-Mississippi West. Multiple native nations were fighting over pastures, river valleys and trade opportunities. During his youth, Crazy Horse was known as Curly Hair. His lighter complexion set him apart, and relatives described him as "Full of fire." (Hamalainen, Pekka, 2022) (www.smitsonianmag.com).

Curly Hair received his military training from his father. His first documented battle experience involved striking an enemy combatant with a stick. His reputation as a fierce warrior grew in subsequent conflicts. Dedicated to protecting the Oglala tribe, in 1865 Crazy Horse earned membership in the elite Shirt Wearers' Society. (Hamalainen, Pekka, 2022).

Crazy Horse enjoyed a strong reputation for outfoxing his adversaries. Despite his shrewdness, he had a reputation as a humble, introverted, man predisposed to low moods and self-doubt. He did not dress extravagantly, and he often avoided social gatherings. (Hamalainen, Pekka, 2022). Though he was considered a great warrior for his people, he chose to never wear a war bonnet.

## **The Great Spirit**

Crazy Horse personified the warrior spirit. Mystical, analytically keen, charitable with his belongings, and fearless in battle, he was dedicated to helping the Lakota preserve their sovereignty and traditional way of living. His leadership during intense battles across the northern Great Plains cemented his legacy as one of the greatest indigenous combat leaders. Short Feather, an Oglala elder, told an American anthropologist that the Crazy Horse period had been "more like the Great Spirits than any other of mankind." (Hamalainen, Pekka, 2022).

**Notable Battles**

By the mid-1870s, Crazy Horse had been fighting for more than a decade for the Lakota Nation. During hostile encounters with the U.S. Army, he had blocked railroad surveys, killed invading settlers, and inspired fellow warriors. Two battles that stood out:

*Battle of Red Buttes:*

The Battle of Red Buttes, Wyoming occurred on July 26, 1865, between U.S. Soldiers and the Cheyenne and Sioux. Five supply wagons began moving eastward down the telegraph road near the North Platte River. The next morning, the army supply train met a detachment of the Ohio Cavalry, past Red Buttes, who warned them that thousands of Indians were besieging the station just ahead and urged them to turn back. (Alexander, Kathy, 2022) (www.legandsofamerica.com).

The commanding sergeant refused; a decision that proved to be a deadly error. U.S. Army soldiers found themselves overwhelmed by natives. The sergeant ordered the wagons corralled and fired upon the attacking Indians. Though hopelessly outnumbered, armed forces held out for four hours. In the end, every one of them would die. The estimated losses to the Indians were 12 killed and 18 wounded. Of the 26 soldiers, only three scouts survived. (Alexander, Kathy, 2022).

*The Fetterman Fight;*

William Judd Fetterman was an Army officer who led his men into this shocking massacre. Fetterman was a Civil War hero who went West and acted a bit too brashly against the Plains Indians. (McCune, B.F., and Hart, 1997) (www.historynet.com).

U. S. soldiers knew that the gold fields of Montana Territory were extremely valuable. To travel from the East to the gold fields, the shortest route was to take the old Oregon Trail to Fort Laramie (southeastern Wyoming) and then pick up the Bozeman Trail. Sioux leaders were upset because the route passed through their buffalo ranges. Native Americans became even more upset when soldiers began to build Camp Connor, later followed by the establishment of Ft. Kearney. (McCune, B.F., and Hart, Louis, 1997).

700 American soldiers were sent to guard the Bozeman Trail. Fetterman had little respect for the fighting ability of Native Americans, openly arguing that a company of regulars could whip a thousand, and a regiment could whip the whole array of hostile tribes.

On the day of the Fetterman fight, as many as 2,000 Natives were waiting in ambush on the far side of Lodge Trail Ridge. Fetterman defied an order not to pursue the Natives over Lodge Trail Ridge. Just as Fetterman's troops reached the Peno Valley, an enormous force of Indians rose from the high grass. Following a fierce 40-minute battle, Fetterman and all 80 of the men in his command were dead. (McCune, B.F. and Hart, Louis, 1997).

In the Battle of Red Buttes, the Fetterman Fight, the Wagon Box Fight, and many others, Crazy Horse planned distinctive maneuvers using craftiness, cunning battle tactics designed to confuse the opponent.

## **Little Big Horn**

In 1874, an Army expedition led by Lt. Col. George Armstrong Custer found gold in the Black Hills of South Dakota. The Black Hills was the property of the Sioux Nation, under a treaty signed six years before. The U.S. government tried to buy the hills, but the Sioux, considering them sacred ground, refused to sell. In 1876, federal troops were dispatched to defeat the Natives and force them onto reservations. (Powers, Thomas, 2010). (www.smithsoniammag.com).

That June, Custer attacked an encampment of Sioux, Cheyenne, and Arapaho on the Little Bighorn River, in what is now Montana. (Powers, Thomas, 2010). Neither Custer nor the 209 men in his immediate command survived the day. Of about 400 soldiers on the hilltop, 53 were killed and 60 were wounded before the Indians ended their siege the next day. (Powers, Thomas, 2010). In total, of the 700 plus U.S. troops at Little Bighorn, 263 died. George Armstrong Custer, commander of the Seventh Cavalry, perished with his men. The massacre infuriated and alarmed the Army. (Powers, Thomas, 2010).

The battle along the Little Bighorn River is universally acknowledged as Crazy Horse's finest moment as a leader. (Mark, Joshua, 2024)) According to oral historical reports of indigenous people who participated in the battle, Crazy Horse executed many daring tactical maneuvers. One such move was to ride hard nearly a mile downriver with his band of warriors to contain and devastate the American cavalrymen. Another tactical movement of legend involved Crazy Horse using himself as bait to lure the cavalry into a dangerous trap.

**Death of Crazy Horse**

Despite the decisive victory at Little Big Horn, Lakota resistance weakened. After continued intermittent fighting, Crazy Horse finally surrendered on May 6, 1877, at Camp Robinson in Nebraska. While in custody, a U.S. Army guard bayoneted Crazy Horse after he allegedly began a skirmish with the soldiers who had arrested him. Crazy Horse died from the wound at just 37 years old. (Powers, Thomas, 2010).

Crazy Horse is proudly judged to be among the most admired Native American leaders. Many Lakota people still view him as someone who reluctantly answered the call to serve. He is revered for his courage, leadership, and his tenacious spirit in the face of unenviable probabilities. Crazy Horse continues to inspire generations as a symbol of resilience and defiance. His legacy is celebrated at the Crazy Horse Memorial, an uncompleted monument sculpture located in the Black Hills, not far from Mount Rushmore.

❖ *__Confirmed Rogue Justice Warrior__*

Crazy Horse, one of the most influential and trailblazing Native men in American history, was highly provocative, yet insanely impactful.

# DR. MARTIN LUTHER KING

*"The ultimate measure of a man is not where he stands in moments of comfort and convenience, but where he stands at times of challenge and controversy."*

Martin Luther King, Jr., a Baptist pastor and social activist, sought equality and human rights for Negroes, the economically disadvantaged, and all victims of injustice thru peaceful protests www.history.com. He organized nonviolent resistance movements, influenced monumental actions and decisions, and delivered his famous "I Have a Dream" speech in 1963 during the historic March on Washington (www.civilrightsmuseum.org).

## **Dr. King's Philosophy**

Martin Luther King visualized a diverse America where all people enjoyed the benefits of equality. Never giving in to fear, he chose courage and determination when fighting for civil rights in the face of oppression, ignorance, and hostility www.history.com. He refused to allow prison, violence, or the threat of death sway his mission. MLK Jr. stood behind his goal of achieving rights for all through nonviolent protests (www.civilrightsmuseum.org).

Dr. King understood the impact of unifying the masses in the push for one common goal. Collectively, he and other civil rights activists could affect policies and influence change nationwide. He realized that violent retaliation would play into the hands of the opposition. Because of this, he advocated nonviolence and taking the high road in all operational processes (www.history.com).

## Montgomery Bus Boycott

The King family was living in Montgomery, Alabama when the segregated city became the epicenter of the fight for civil rights in America. The crusade was roused by the landmark Brown v. Board of Education decision of 1954.

On December 1, 1955, Rosa Parks, an employee of the local chapter of the National Association for the Advancement of Colored People (NAACP), was arrested when she refused to give up her seat to a white passenger on a Montgomery public bus. Activists coordinated a boycott of the city bus system that would last for 381 days (www.history.com). A reduction in the number of paying customers placed a severe economic strain on the public transit system. Dr. Martin Luther King Jr., chosen as the protest's leader and official spokesman, was beginning to gain national notoriety and prominence.

## Southern Christian Leadership Conference

Encouraged by the triumph of the Montgomery Bus Boycott, in 1957, King and other civil rights activists (many of whom were fellow ministers) established the Southern Christian Leadership Conference (SCLC). The SCLC was a group committed to achieving full equality for African Americans through nonviolent protest (www.nationalsclc.org).

In his role as SCLC president, Martin Luther King Jr. traveled across the country and around the world, giving lectures on nonviolent protest and civil rights. King was networking with religious figures, activists, and political leaders. The SCLC motto was "Not one hair of one head of one person should be harmed." Dr. King remained at the helm of this influential organization until his death (www.nationalsclc.org).

## Letter from Birmingham Jail

In 1960, King and his family moved to his native Atlanta, where he joined his father as co-pastor of the Ebenezer Baptist Church. The SCLC was increasingly prominent in the battle for civil rights throughout the decade. The philosophy of nonviolence was put to a severe test during the Birmingham campaign of 1963. Boycotts, sit-ins, and marches to protest segregation and unfair hiring practices became the organizations (SCLC) primary tactics.

While incarcerated at the city jail, King wrote a civil rights manifesto known as the "Letter from Birmingham Jail." The letter is a well-known defense of the notion of civil disobedience. King was steadfast in his beliefs about refusing to obey laws which are immoral or unjust (Tearle, Dr Oliver, 2024). Dr. King made a powerful argument for obeying a higher moral law rather than manmade laws. Interestingly, he also embraced the term "extremist," observing that some of the most pious and peaceful figures in history have been 'extremists' of one kind of another (Tearle, Dr. Oliver, 2024).

## March on Washington and I Have a Dream Speech

The March on Washington of 1963 was the largest gathering for civil rights of its time. An estimated 250,000 people attended the rally that was designed to shed light on the injustices Black Americans continued to face across the country. This event is considered a watershed moment in American history (www.nps.gov).

The March on Washington culminated in Dr. King's most famous oration, known as the "I Have a Dream" speech. Standing on the steps of the Lincoln Memorial (a monument to the president who brought down the institution of slavery in the United States a century prior), King shared his vision of a future in which "this nation will rise and live out the true meaning of its creed (www.history.com).

The "I Have a Dream" speech cemented King's reputation at home and overseas. He was named "Man of the Year" by TIME magazine, and in 1964, became the youngest person ever awarded the Nobel Peace Prize.

## Selma March

The Selma to Montgomery march was part of a series of civil rights protests that occurred in 1965. The march took place in Alabama, a Southern state with deeply entrenched racist policies. As the world watched, the protesters—under the protection of federalized National Guard troops—achieved their goal, walking for three days to reach Montgomery, Alabama (www.history.com).

The marchers did not get far before State police rushed the group at the Edmund Pettus Bridge and beat them back toward Selma with whips, nightsticks, and tear gas. Upon viewing this scene on television, many Americans became enraged. Civil rights and religious leaders of all faiths rushed to Selma in protest. President Lyndon B. Johnson sent federal troops to keep the peace. That August, Congress passed the Voting Rights Act, which guaranteed the right to vote—first awarded by the 15$^{th}$ Amendment—to all African Americans (www.history.com).

## Assassination of Dr. Martin Luther King, Jr.

The events in Selma deepened a growing rift between Martin Luther King Jr. and young radicals who repudiated his nonviolent methods and his commitment to working within the established political framework (www.civilrightsmuseum.org). More militant Black leaders began to rise in prominence, King broadened the scope of his activism to address issues such as the Vietnam War and poverty among Americans of all races. In 1967, King and the SCLC embarked on an ambitious program known as the Poor People's Campaign, which was to include a massive march on the capital.

On the evening of April 4, 1968, Martin Luther King was assassinated. He was fatally shot while standing on the balcony of a motel in Memphis, where King had traveled to support a sanitation workers' strike. In the aftermath of his death, a wave of rioting swept major cities across the country. President Lyndon Johnson declared a National Day of Mourning.

In 1983, President Ronald Reagan signed a bill creating a U.S. federal holiday in honor of King. Observed on the third Monday of January, Martin Luther King Day was first celebrated in 1986.

- ❖ ***<u>Confirmed Rogue Justice Warrior</u>***

    Dr. Martin Luther King, one of the most influential and trailblazing men in American history, was highly controversial, yet insanely impactful.

# WINSTON CHURCHILL

Winston Churchill was born on November 30, 1874, in Oxfordshire, England. He was known as a British statesman, orator, and author. As Prime Minister (1940–45, 1951–55) he rallied the British people during World War II and led his country from the brink of defeat to victory (www.britannica.com) 2024.

### Youthful Years

The young Churchill suffered an unhappy and sadly neglected childhood. Following a poor academic record, he decided to pursue a military career in the British army. It took three attempts before he was able to pass the entrance examination to the Royal Military College (www.biography.com). He served as a soldier and a journalist. In 1899, at the age of 25, Churchill resigned from his military commission to begin a career in politics and writing.

Even as a young adult, Winston Churchill was known for his self-confidence and boyish charm. He excelled in writing and delivering a prepared speech. Churchill was beginning to earn a reputation for erratic judgement (www.britannica.com). Radical elements in his political nature came to light due to the encouragement of two well-known colleagues.

### Early Political Adventures

Winston Churchill enjoyed a sensational rise to prominence in national politics before World War I. His theatrical attacks on the House of Lords were vigorous and savage. He is credited with bringing the British Navy to instant readiness, and he gained the largest naval expenditure in his country's history. At the same time, Churchill attempted to curb political power, causing some to label him a traitor. He won widespread popular acclaim for his courage and fearlessness. Churchill treasured dramatic action, but his acerbic language and gruff demeanor caused him to pay a heavy political price. Churchill was building a reputation as both a rebel and a resistor.

## World War I

The first world war tested Winston Churchill's capacity. His efforts have been assessed to be robust but full of dissension. Churchill served active duty in France. In 1915, he proceeded militarily against the wishes of his command, which caused him to come under heavy criticism. In 1917, Churchill was instrumental in the developmental production of battle tanks. In 1919, he became Secretary of War. In this role, he significantly cut military expenditures.

## From 1922-1939

Winston Churchill found himself in and out of office many times during this period of his life. He survived financially by using his writing skills. Noted economist John Maynard Keynes scathingly criticized him when he led a movement to restore the gold standard. The controversial economic maneuver led to high unemployment and monetary depreciation. Churchill found himself distrusted by every political party. Before doubting opposition, he argued tirelessly that Britian must take a looming German threat seriously (www.winstonchurchill.org).

## Leadership During WW II

Winston Churchill was known as a passionate patriot. He believed in Great Britian's prominence, and in its consequence in world affairs. He was known as a man of iron constitution who thrived on calamity and immediacy.

As Prime Minister, in Churchill's first speech to the House of Commons, he warned the Country of the hard road ahead. He famously told his nation that "I have nothing to offer but blood, toil, tears and sweat" (www.winstonchurchill.org). He committed himself, and his nation, to WWII until victory was achieved. Churchill was able to recruit his indispensable ally, the United States, to help with the war effort.

The decisive Battle of Britian began in July 10, 1940. Churchill was well suited for the role. He alternately was on the firing line—at fight headquarters, inspecting coast defenses or antiaircraft batteries, visiting scenes of bomb damage or victims of the air campaign. Smoking his cigar, giving his V sign, or broadcasting frank reports to the nation, laced with touches of his famous Churchillian humor splashed with Churchillian rhetoric. Praising British spirit and resolve, Churchill famously declared "This was their finest hour." (www.winstonchurchill.org).

Winston Churchill was instrumental in the codification of the British-US wartime alliance. Churchill was quoted as saying "Give us the tools and we'll finish the job." Churchill was the primary architect behind the formation of the coalition that was known as the "grand alliance." The grand alliance included Great Britian, the Soviet Union, and the United States. The pooling of military and economic resources, and successful collaboration, is widely credited with being the turning point that led to allied victory.

### Electoral Downfall

In 1944, victory for the allied forces seemed imminent. But, party politics in Great Britian were at a fever pitch. Churchill's political opposition demanded that the Country hold a national election. As popular leader of his country's war effort, Churchill was thought by many to be unbeatable. His political opposition smartly focused on economic and social reform. In 1945, the British people ultimately decided Churchill's flamboyance and edginess, though perfect for wartime, was not best for their immediate domestic future. Churchill saw his party's influence reduced. He was forced to relinquish his position as Prime Minister and accept the role of leader of the parliamentary opposition.

### Post War

The general election of February 1950 afforded Churchill an opportunity to again seek his personal agenda. He campaigned within the confines of his party's platform. His political party gained much renewed power, but it took a second election in 1951 to restore them to control. Following the gains at the ballot box, Churchill became British Minister for the second time. He received two notable awards, the Order of the Garter, and the Nobel Prize for Literature.

In 1953 Churchill suffered a stroke which caused partial paralysis. Though he mostly recovered, he was never the same. In 1954, on his 80$^{th}$ birthday, Churchill was honored with a ceremony of tribute and affection in Westminster Hall. In 1955, he resigned as Prime Minister.

## **Retirement and Death**

Winston Churchill published another major work, *A History of the English- Speaking Peoples*, four volumes (1956–58). But his health was declining, and his public appearances became rare. On April 9, 1963, he received the unique distinction of having an honorary U.S. citizenship conferred on him by an act of Congress. His death at his London home in January 1965 was followed by a state funeral at which most of the world paid tribute.

❖ ***Confirmed Rogue Justice Warrior***

Sir Winston Churchill, considered by many to be architect of Allied victory in the war to end all wars (WWII), was highly controversial, yet insanely impactful

# DONALD J. TRUMP

Donald J. Trump was the 45th, and currently the 47th President of the United States. Trump lost his bid for reelection to former vice president Joe Biden following his first term. Trump has been accused in numerous scandals, was impeached twice, and became the first former president to be indicted and convicted of criminal charges. However, he also is known for many significant accomplishments, and he engineered perhaps the greatest political comeback of all time when he won Presidential re-election in November, 2024.

### Early Years

Donald Trump was born in 1946 to a wealthy family in Queens, New York. Described as an energetic, assertive child, the teenage Trump was sent to attend the New York Military Academy. In this highly structured environment, he found success both academically and athletically. As a young adult, Trump attended the Wharton School of Finance at the University of Pennsylvania. He graduated with a degree in economics in 1968.

### Business Career

Trump followed his father into a career in real estate development. He has long held a reputation as a daring idealist with grand ambitions. His business ventures have included the Trump Organization, Trump Tower, casinos in Atlantic City and television franchises like The Apprentice and Miss Universe. Trump has business agreements throughout the world. He is also known as the proprietor of the Trump National Doral and Mar-a-Lago golf courses. He earns income from merchandise and royalties from two books, *The Art of the Deal* and *Crippled America: How to Make America Great Again*.

## Presidential Successes Attributed to Donald Trump

- Unemployment rate reached 3.5 percent, the lowest in a half-century. Unemployment for women hit its lowest rate in nearly 70 years
- Rebuilt the United States military with over $2.2 trillion in defense spending, including $738 billion for 2020.
- Established the Space Force, the first new branch of the United States Armed Forces since 1947
- Brought jobs, factories, and industries back to the USA. Put in place policies to bring back supply chains from overseas
- Defeated Isis caliphate
- Initiated criminal justice reform with First Step Act
- Record high stock market numbers and record 401ks
- Ended the North American Free Trade Agreement (NAFTA), and replaced it with the United States-Mexico-Canada Agreement (USMCA)
- United States became number one producer of oil and natural gas in the world www.trumpwhitehousearchives.gov).

## Foreign Affairs

As with every aspect of his Presidency, Donald Trump's foreign affairs activity simultaneously garnered a great deal of praise, and wide criticism. Some of the more deliberated actions include:

- Suspended the Intermediate-Range Nuclear Forces Treaty with Russia, due to repeated violations of the agreement
- Ordered military strike upon a Syrian airfield in response to a chemical attack. Participated in a second strike with Great Britian and France
- Killed terrorist Abu Bakr al-Baghdadi following an American commando raid
- Imposed sanctions on steel and aluminum that impacted world trade
- Imposed sanctions on China that led to a $200 billion purchase of American products by the Chinese
- Recognized Jerusalem as the capital of Israel and new site of the American embassy

- Withdrew U.S. from an Iranian nuclear deal
- Carried out military strikes against Iran, and killed terrorist leader Qassem Soleimani with a drone strike
- Summit, threats, and neutralization of Kim Jong-un of North Korea

## **Mueller Investigation**

Former federal prosecutor and FBI director Robert Mueller was selected to serve as a special counsel to lead an investigation into Russian meddling in the 2016 presidential election and possible ties to the Trump campaign. Some 3-years later, Mueller submitted his report to the Attorney General. The report indicated that there was no evidence of collusion between the Trump campaign and Russian agents. Some former Trump associates were indicted because of the probe.

## **Impeachment**

A Democratic majority in the House of Representatives voted to proceed with two articles of impeachment, charging the President with abuse of power and obstruction of Congress. Eight days later, Donald Trump became only the third U.S. President to be impeached. The House voted along party lines for the two articles of impeachment. The trial formally came to an end when the United States Senate voted, mostly along party lines, to acquit President Trump on both charges.

On January 6, 2021, a large group of protestors descended upon the Capitol to protest what they believed were voting irregularities. The Capitol was stormed, people fought with law enforcement. Some illegally entered the Capitol and took over a Senate chamber. One woman was shot and killed by a Capitol Police officer.

Political opponents accused President Trump of encouraging and inciting a riot. Trump issued a statement shortly after the event which read: "Even though I totally disagree with the outcome of the election, and the facts bear me out, nevertheless there will be an orderly transition on January 20$^{th}$."

On January 13, 2020, the Democratic majority in the House of Representatives voted to impeach Trump for a second time for incitement of insurrection. This historic action made Donald Trump the first president in American history to be impeached twice. On February 13, Donald Trump was again found not guilty in the Senate, with a vote of 57-43 to acquit.

On July 13, 2024, a lone gunman attempted to assassinate Donald Trump as he spoke at a Presidential campaign rally in Butler, Pennsylvania. Trump was struck by a bullet on his right ear. Secret Service agents successfully removed Trump from the event and helped him obtain medical treatment. Trump survived the attempt, and continued his campaign.

On September 16, 2024, another potential assassin stalked Presidential candidate Trump while he was playing golf at the Mar-A-Lago course in Florida. A U.S. Secret Service agent foiled the plot when he spotted the potential gunmen. The suspect was subsequently arrested and incarcerated. Donald Trump survived and continued his Presidential campaign.

Donald J. Trump was elected President of the United States for a second time in November, 2024.

❖ *<u>Confirmed Rogue Justice Warrior</u>*

President Donald J. Trump is loved by some, loathed by others. Donald Trump is highly controversial, yet insanely impactful.

# MORE CONFIRMED ROGUE JUSTICE WARRIORS

This chapter highlights seven **Rogue Justice Warriors** who defied expectations, challenged oppression, and redefined the world. However, the list of influencers who used Rogue Justice Warrior behavior to attain greatness, could go on-and-on, almost endlessly. History is crystal clear; the greatest, most prominent individuals in the world embody exactly what we previously identified as Rogue Justice Warrior attributes.

It is not coincidental that the best of the best share many commonalities. All that follow are known for multiple significant accomplishments, and multiple controversial activities. These Rogue Justice Warriors, through their defiant transformational qualities also left an indelible mark on history:

Theodore Roosevelt, Spartacus, Nelson Mandela, Napolean Boneparte, Mahatma Ghandi, Abraham Lincoln, Susan B. Anthony, Moses, Andrew Jackson, Alexander the Great, Joan of Arc, Thomas Jefferson, Ben Franklin, Klaus Von Stauffenberg, Genghis Khan, Cleopatra, Muhammad, Samuel Adams, John Hancock, John F. Kennedy, Jair Bolsonaro, Christopher Columbus, Augustas (Julius) Ceasar, Robert F. Kennedy.

## **CONCLUSION**

Civilization has always been filled with legendary overachievers who attained greatness primarily due to who they were, and what they did. I encourage you to analyze and reflect upon the protagonist listed in this chapter. All believed passionately in something bigger than their individuality. They all rowed upstream against established societal norms. Strong-minded and gutsy, Rogue Justice Warriors are willing to suffer personal distress (ridicule, imprisonment, or death) when they believe they can achieve spectacular, life altering results. They personify renown and controversy.

# MORE CONFIRMED ROGUE JUSTICE WARRIORS

Rogue Justice Warriors are principled, admirable, unafraid, and motivational. Determined to "Do something about it, because something needs to be done," they combine defiance and non-compliance with decisiveness and self-assurance. Firm and clear thinking, RJW's are determined to construct and follow the virtuous path of their belief system. Rogue Justice Warriors are mentally tough, and make their own rules. The magnetic appeal, cunning, and persuasiveness of a Rogue Justice Warrior makes them effective with multiple audiences.

# Chapter 7

## *WHEN YOU'RE RIGHT, YOU FIGHT*

*"One man with courage makes a majority"*

**President Andrew Jackson**

We have invested significant time exploring how rogue mentality and behavior can be the key to lionhearted achievement—true preeminence. The illustrious protagonist examples examined in the preceding chapter illuminate how much Rogue Justice Warriors can accomplish. While the great among us make compelling case studies, it is equally important to examine how each of us can excel by embracing our individual rogueness when appropriate.

### CAN THE AVERAGE PERSON BE A ROGUE JUSTICE WARRIOR

Though I realize that the definition of being a pre-eminent person is subjective, I suspect that most would agree that the pinnacle performers among us account for only a small fraction of the population. There is great value in using the best of the best to make the point that ***we need rogue justice now more than ever!*** Evolution of the overarching theme leads me to wonder; how does the Rogue Justice Warrior phenomena relate to the average person? Can the man or woman leading a normal life find success by being a Rogue Justice Warrior?

I offer my personal stories as an attempt to open the reader to the probability that Rogue Justice Warriors emerge from everyday people living ordinary lives. As you read some of my experiences, I encourage you to contemplate how personal challenges in your life have influenced who you are today.

## **SETTING THE BACK STORY**

In the late 1950's, a young, 19-year-old mother delivered her second child. The male baby joined a sister who had been born only 11-months prior. Dad was working to support the family, and he was going to college at night. Mom, a spoiled teenager herself, had two babies less than a year old at home. It is not hard to imagine the frustrations and challenges all were about to endure.

Family members have relayed that the young mother struggled to cope with a highly stressful situation. Relatives stepped up to try and help the family get by, but frustration, depression, and resentment entered the picture from an early juncture. At a very young age, I can remember being a rebellious child that resisted my mother's directions. It seemed that I was continuously in trouble, being corrected and punished at every turn. The stage was set for dismal difficulty.

Mom was determined that she was going to win the battle of wills with her hard-headed boy. By the time that I was a few years old, I had a lot of experience undergoing physical and emotional abuse from my mother. I can remember many instances of whacking, hitting me with any item within arm's reach. She would literally pick up whatever was near and hit me with it, all while hurling hurtful and degrading remarks when she was angry.

At this stage of my life, I had a severe speech impediment (stuttering), in addition to other emotional ailments. Some might argue that these childhood difficulties had no connection to the abuse that I was experiencing, but my belief is that there was most certainly a relationship.

## **FIRST TIME THAT I RECALL GOING ROGUE**

To this day, I remember one incident as clearly as if it happened yesterday. I was somewhere between 6-7 years old. Though

I have no idea what was the cause of the unrest, my mother was mad with me per usual. Full of fury, she charged at me. I attempted to flee, but she cornered me in the family room of our home. Somehow, I ended up on the floor. Screaming vitriol, she was stomping my head and body while I lay, cowering to cover up.

In that moment, something inside me changed. To protect myself, I determinedly got to my feet. She was holding me in place as she continued the hitting and the degradation. I remember looking her directly in the eye, and thinking to myself, "STOP IT, NOW." I said nothing, but in my mind, I was resolutely thinking "If you do not stop hurting me, I am going to fight back to protect myself. "I will hurt you if I have to, that will make it stop." I remember that my will was iron-clad, strong as steel, and I meant exactly what I was thinking. Enough was enough!

My mother suddenly ceased the abuse, and released my arm. I will never forget the look on her face. It was clear that she had read my facial expressions and body language. She knew what was on my mind. She turned and walked away from me. Though she did continue to use fleshly and condescending punishment throughout my youth, she never physically abused me from that day forward.

Though just a very young child, this lesson taught me that standing up against injustice—no matter how young or powerless one may seem—can create real change. As you shall see, it is a lesson that has been repeated throughout my life.

## **MORE ROGUE LESSONS FROM CHILDHOOD**

My next memorable rogue experience occurred when I was a 12-year-old seventh grader in middle school. In class, while working on an art project, another student deliberately and maliciously destroyed my work. Instinctually, I stood up, reached across the table, and punched my so-called friend in the face. He went flying backwards as I had knocked him out of his chair. He was laying on the classroom floor holding his nose and crying.

Blood was flowing freely; it turned out that I broke his nose with the punch.

The male teacher decided that I should be punished. He offered me the option of reporting the incident to my parents or taking three (3) licks from him and his wooden paddle. I chose the corporal punishment, telling him sarcastically to bring it. In front of the entire class, I took the 3-licks from the teacher, making cocky, smart-aleck comments after each blow.

The incident was resolved, but I learned a lesson. The point of this story is not to advocate for physical violence; however, I felt completely justified in standing up for myself and correcting a wrong. Sometimes righteousness has a price, and we must be willing to pay the price to make things acceptable.

*Basketball*

I grew up in a State where basketball was king. I had two uncles who were basketball stars, and I felt I was next in line. My young career was going well, and it looked like I was on my way to stardom. An assistant coach at my school went out of his way to meet with me one-on-one, telling me that "I had what it took, and that I was going to make it if I continued to work hard."

Unfortunately, I was experiencing a medical problem while playing ball. Back pain was with me every moment of every practice. Gave it all I had, but I struggled thru every session. I was in so much pain that I was forced to go home and lay down for an hour or two after practice before I could change clothes. I could not even take my shoes off by myself. Despite it all, I passionately continued to play thru the agony.

For some reason, the coach of the team(s) felt that I was faking the injury. He ridiculed and belittled me constantly for 3-full seasons. He called me lazy (the nicest language that he used), and he continuously pointed out to my teammates that I was not providing full effort. Though I had communicated to the coach that

I was injured, and that my family was seeking medical diagnosis from doctors, it did not matter.

I suppose the coach thought that he was motivational, but the effect was quite the opposite. Finally, after 3-full years of nasty ill-treatment, I felt that enough was enough. After one public bullying firestorm, I lashed out at the coach in my own defense. I responded to the coach's venom by saying "Fuck you, I am hurt. You are an asshole. I do not have to take this shit from you." My unsophisticated approach did not go over well with the coach.

In the off-season following my flareup, a team of doctors diagnosed my back condition. I underwent major spinal fusion surgery on my back, taking a full 9-months to recover. The following pre-season, that same coach (who had now moved up the ranks), cut me from the team during tryouts. Everyone in the school was shocked, we all knew (including the coach) that I was one of the best players at the school.

The reality was that there was no way that the coach was going to let the kid that talked ugly to him make the squad. The primary lesson, standing up for yourself and fighting back can extract a heavy price. Though I was completely right in what I said, the consequences were severe. My basketball career ended that day, and I lost my dream. Again, I felt validated, but the price of seeking justice proved excruciatingly harsh.

## **TEENAGE ADULT ROGUE**

One sunny afternoon three friends called and asked me (I had just turned 18-years-old) to join them in a pick-up basketball game. I enthusiastically accepted the invitation and promptly climbed into the back seat of a car being driven by a roundball acquaintance. As we became mobile, the driver of the vehicle produced a full-face Halloween mask. One of the friends suggested that we have some fun and see whom we could scare with the mask.

Wearing the mask, a baseball hat, and with a cigarette in his mouth, the driver of the vehicle began to approach various people, grunting and groaning at them. None of us ever considered that our playground was a strip-mall parking lot. A bank teller at a drive thru window of the local bank was not amused. Unbeknown to the pranksters, the bank teller called 911 and reported that four men with masks and guns were about to rob the bank.

Within minutes, countless police vehicles, with emergency equipment activated, converged on the "*suspect*" vehicle. More than ten officers surrounded the vehicle and aggressively confronted the teens. With their weapons deployed, some officers were yelling "Put your hands on the roof of the car." Other officers were screaming "Don't move, or I'll blow your brains out." After much confusion, the officers pulled me out of the vehicle, slammed me over the trunk, handcuffed me behind my back, and forcefully threw me onto the ground face first.

Upon arrival at the police substation and subsequent interrogation, the police realized that the four youthful offenders never tried to rob a bank. However, local law enforcement was angry that foolish teens had endangered the public and wasted police time and resources. I was arrested and charged with one misdemeanor count of disorderly conduct.

A magistrate set a ridiculously high bond to "punish" this fresh-faced eighteen-year-old. Incarceration followed in the city jail. Physical safety, filth, sexual propositioning, dignity, and psychological health all came to the forefront of my existence as I confronted incarceration. My father had to put up our home as collateral to get me released from jail.

Against the advice of my attorney, I refused to accept a "guilty" plea bargain offered by the prosecutor. Though I had no experience with the court system, I felt strongly that I was only guilty of riding in the back seat of a car. Threatened with the likelihood of a 12-month jail sentence, I stood tenaciously by my belief that justice would prevail if I fought for it and publicly told my story.

My attorney shook his head at me and said "Boy, you are a fool. If you go before a judge, you are going to jail for a year." I refused to change my stance. My lawyer left that pre-court meeting shaking his head in disbelief. About 20-minutes later the same lawyer, my attorney, returned to the meeting room with his hand extended. He shook my hand, saying "I don't know how you did it."

Against judicious probability, the prosecuting attorney abruptly and unexpectedly reversed course. The criminal charge against me was dismissed. I said, "You're damn right," as I left the courthouse and went home to continue my life. This court victory reinforced my belief that resistance against long odds and fighting for what you believe in is where justice can be found. The courage and pugnacity behind sticking to my principles allowed me to protect my criminal record.

## **CAREER ROGUE**

The interval immediately following arrest, incarceration, and court process caused me to be very dissatisfied with the criminal justice system. After a few years of recuperating and contemplating my options, I made a conscious decision to fashion success from adversity. I decided to seek a law enforcement career upon realizing that I could have enormous impact by joining the police business and influencing the actions of those in the system.

I ultimately enjoyed a terrific, nearly 30-year law enforcement career. However, just as with everything else in life, all was not peaches and cream. Although there were **MANY** times that I chose to go rogue and fight for what was right regarding my career, I will recount only two instances for this book.

### *Pre-hire fight*

During the final stage of my law enforcement job hunt, the hiring agency required all applicants to successfully complete a physical examination. For many years, one Doctor had the exclusive contract. The doctor had me disrobe and wear a gown that was open in the rear. During my exam, the doctor, who was alone with me, turned out the lights and told me to walk across the room away from him. The doctor was shining a flashlight as I walked. I had no idea what this exercise had to do with an employment physical exam, but I complied as directed because I was young, naïve, and I wanted the job!

Another of the examination tasks involved an eye exam. The doctor asked me to identify a number within a set of colored dots on a cardboard prop. I did not do very well on this test, as I had much trouble seeing the hidden numbers. Upon completion of other assessments, the doctor told me to get dressed and meet him in his office.

Once alone in his office, the doctor informed me that he was not going to recommend my hire to the agency. The doctor told me flatly that I was red-green colorblind, and therefore he could not endorse my employment. I disagreed with the doctor's assessment and vehemently objected to his analysis. He proceeded to offer two examples to buttress his point 1) He asked me "What color is the top light on a traffic signal?" When I answered, red, he said "See, you do not really see the light as red, you have just learned that the color is red." 2) The doctor then asked "What color is grass?" I replied, green. His response was "See, you don't really see that as green, you have only learned from others that grass is green."

Befuddled, and fearing for my future career, I chose to stand up for myself. I picked up a magazine from the doctor's desk and flipped haphazardly thru the pages. When I found something red in the magazine, I pointed it out to the doctor and said, "This is red." I did the same when I found a random item that was green. The doctor rebuffed my declarations, and said "Son, when your wife tells you that that you are wearing one brown sock and one black sock, you had better believe her and change your socks."

Fighting for my future career, I protested the doctor's error to the police hiring manager. Ultimately, I went to an ophthalmologist for a higher-level exam. The ophthalmologist displayed a red light and a green light in his office. When I correctly identified the colors, the ophthalmologist stated "You're not red-green color-blind." I took the results to the hiring manager, after which I got the job and enjoyed a full career.

Again, I was forced to fight a high-stakes battle against unfairness. Many years later, the doctor was identified as a degenerate deviant. He lost his medical license and was forced to give up his medical career.

## Battles with the CEO

My law enforcement career was going very well. After just 3 ½ years as a uniform officer, I was transferred to the detective division. Though not a promotion, this assignment was considered advancement, and was known as a stepping stone for future opportunities. Following a 2-year stint as a detective, I was promoted to Sergeant. Six (6) years later, I was promoted to Lieutenant. Following a few short assignments as a Lieutenant, I was promoted to Captain - a command staff position. I was enjoying much work success. All was well with my career, then suddenly it went south.

One year into my role as a commander, the new Chief of Police called me to a closed-door meeting. The Chief told me what he wanted, and told me to complete the task. What the Chief asked me to do was unethical and highly improper, though technically not illegal. I politely declined the assignment. I told the Chief that I was sorry, but that I could not implement the directive. I indicated that the ask was inappropriate, very much outside my comfort zone as an ethical leader.

Just as you might guess, the Chief was not happy with my response. He absolutely exploded with anger, yelling & cursing at me. He told me that I was not a team player, that I was insubordinate, and that I was a traitor. The Chief then furiously threw me out of his office. From that moment forward, he waged a relentless campaign to sabotage my career.

Over the course of the next 10-months, the Chief and I battled at every intersection. At one point the CEO put his finger in my face and angrily said "I'm going to get you." Things got so bad that work peers were approaching me privately asking "What is wrong, clearly there is something really wrong between you two." **Many** bad interactions and occurrences followed. I was written up for a fabricated incident that never occurred, and I was transferred punitively against my will.

Finally, after 10-months of bullying and abuse, enough was enough. The Chief had once again called me behind closed doors, cursing and belittling me over some minor perception that he had blown out of proportion. With composure, I put my hand out and forcefully said STOP IT! He looked at me and sarcastically said "You have a problem **BOY**?" I calmly replied in the affirmative, and began to list in detail four of the most egregious incidents that he had perpetrated against me in the previous months. I made it clear to him that he had created a hostile work environment, and I told him that his bad behavior was going to end that day. I further told him that if he did not cease the illegal behavior, that I would meet with his boss, the top Executive, and that "I would kick the fucking doors wide open." I ended the defense of myself by saying "Do you understand me?"

The Chief stated that I had an attitude problem. I replied that he could call it whatever he chose, but that I was not going to continue to put up with his abusive behavior for even one more second. He angrily threw me out of his office. This Chief's bad public deeds toward me ended that very day. He continued to harass, and deny opportunities until he retired, but the necessity of me fighting back brought public relief and ended the bald-faced ill-treatment. There was a heavy price to pay, but I did what needed to be done despite weighty personal risks, and very real consequences.

## THE REASON I SHARED MY STORIES

You will recall that I began this chapter by asking whether an average person can be a Rogue Justice Warrior? I believe that not only is it possible for each of us to go rogue while seeking justice, it is often the only way to get the job done! My hope is that those reading this book will take the call to be a Rogue Justice Warrior to heart. *Righteous anger over malevolence is virtuous.*

Rogue Justice Warriors understand that the battle is often between right and wrong; fighting for justice vs. injustice. There are some things in this world that ought to make us angry. We should be outraged by unfairness, violence, hardship, inequity, injury, and illicit loss of life that runs rampant all around us.

It is my sincere believe that Rogue Justice Warriors blossom from a combination of nature vs. nurture. My personal experience, along with the childhood stories of our featured protagonist, convinces me that Rogue Justice Warriors are born with the vision of an eagle, and the heart of a lion.

Cognitive aptitude is certainly an ingredient of human development, nonetheless, RJW's seem to innately possess something more. The way that they carry themselves exudes the IT factor. Learning and harnessing, I believe that we refine the craft of rogueness thru life experiences. We choose, and apply, the level of fight that comes from within ourselves.

I want to be clear that the examples from my life are not expressed as an attempt to conflate my experiences with those of the great protagonist dissected in Chapter 6. Quite the contrary, I want it to be well absorbed that all of us, average humans, can and must perform as high-level Rogue Justice Warriors.

It is our duty, and my challenge to you, that you take courageous action to nullify maltreatment. Act according to a hardy code of conscience. Rebel against inequitableness. Be brave, bold, and fearless regardless of potential penalties. Scrap valiantly when you believe in the cause. Do not let fear silence your voice, and do not avoid conflict when it is needed.

Be willing to go outside established standards when necessary to propel affirmative transformation. Take shrewd, purposeful gambles when the potential for significance presents itself. Rely on your gut instinct, and resolve problematic things that need to be disentangled. Live the creed, ***"When You're Right, You Fight."*** The risks are real, and the path is often painful, but true justice is not often achieved without a fight!

Heed the call! Rogue Justice Warriors model the biblical scriptural excerpts found in Isaiah (NIV) "Do not fear" and "Here I am, send me."

# Chapter 8

## *THINGS YOU MIGHT HEAR A ROGUE JUSTICE WARRIOR SAY*

- ❖ Honor exists in righteous action, even when it is not allowed
- ❖ Whether others like it or not is not the deciding factor
- ❖ Gutsiness is not just about being fearless—but also knowing when the time is right
- ❖ I do not capitulate to corruption
- ❖ If regulations hold you back, overcome them
- ❖ Do not hide behind illegitimate directives
- ❖ Justice is not about punishment, it is about restoration
- ❖ Sometimes, doing the right thing means breaking inappropriate policies
- ❖ Aw, hell no!
- ❖ The system can be blind, but I see what needs to be done
- ❖ I do not need someone to tell me what is right
- ❖ You do not need permission to seize what is rightfully yours
- ❖ When those in power fail the people, it is up to us to make things right
- ❖ Rebellion can be the highest form of loyalty
- ❖ Integrity is my compass
- ❖ I answer to a higher code
- ❖ I will not bend, I will not splinter, and I will not back down
- ❖ When the law fails, justice demands a new route
- ❖ Nah, we're not doing that
- ❖ Justice is not about laws; it is about doing what is right
- ❖ I fight for the truth, even when others think I am out-of-bounds
- ❖ Break the law if you must to safeguard the principal
- ❖ Sometimes justice is not handed down, it is commandeered
- ❖ True justice is not swayed by politics

## THINGS YOU MIGHT HEAR A ROGUE WARRIOR SAY

- ❖ When laws protect the guilty, it is time to rewrite the law
- ❖ I do hard things that others are afraid to do
- ❖ Silence in the face of injustice, is complicity
- ❖ I would rather be hated for standing up, than loved for staying silent
- ❖ The path to justice does not always follow a straight line
- ❖ Some may say rebellion, I say correction
- ❖ I'm not here to make peace, I'm here to make it right
- ❖ Order without justice is just control
- ❖ Silence never changed anything
- ❖ They know that I can't be bought
- ❖ I scream the truth, sometimes that might hurt

Rogue Justice Warriors are self-assured, strategic, and prepared to outmaneuver unjust obstacles.

# Chapter 9

# ROGUEOMETER

*Everybody has a plan till they get punched in the mouth*

**Mike Tyson**

Boxing champion and notorious tough guy Mike Tyson (certainly a rogue, but not necessarily one whom I would consider a Rogue Justice Warrior), uttered the famous quote above while preparing for a fight with Evander Holyfield. To further our understanding of **Rogue Justice**, I am pilfering the essence of Tyson's statement to create a new sentiment. From your author's standpoint, I transition his quote into *"Most people fancy themselves a fighter until they get punched in the mouth."* How will you respond when you feel pain and/or when you get hurt? "What do I do now," is the question that each of us must answer about our individual rogueness?

The reader's visceral response to my adaptation of Tyson's quote will tell us a lot about just how much rogueness flows through their veins. It is quite easy for us to talk about how rogue we are, uncomplicated to brazenly conversate trash when everything seems to be going our way. However, the intersection of what we say we will do, and what we are truthfully willing to do, is the crucial moment of veritable engagement.

What will you REALLY do when faced with extraordinarily difficult circumstances? If you get knocked down (literally or figuratively), do you lie on the mat licking your wounds, thinking "No more, I'm hurt!" Or, do you immediately bounce back up, thinking something akin to President Donald Trump's "Fight, Fight, Fight!" Does your mind tell you to quit, this tussle is over?

Or, is your brain propelling you toward kicking some ass and getting your pound of flesh?

Human beings get to make choices regarding both their mindset and their psychological toughness. Is your choice some romanticized idea of what you want peers and associates to think? The question of how Rogue Justice Warriors act in response to significant adversity is quite different than any fantasy of good intention. Is your internal constitution the equivalent of brass balls strong? How willing are you to go rogue? I use the term "willing" because I am convinced that one's echelon of rogueness boils down to choice.

*It is obvious that there are times when a fight is literally over, and you cannot continue. There are also some situations where retreat or flight is the best strategic choice. However, those situations are not what we are discussing in this chapter.*

The level of warrior panache will be impacted by culture, personality, sophistication, and internal constitution. In the end, choice still determines how we decide to perform. You do not need to be the biggest, strongest, or meanest to be the most badass champion in the arena.

The crème of the crop radiates mental toughness, nerve, guts, and fierceness. All day, every day. Remember, Rogue Justice Warriors do not shy away when faced with difficulty. When engaged in battle, crafting, attaining, and using the upper hand greatly enhances the chance of success. There can be advantage in having your opponent believe that you might be tough enough – or crazy enough - to implement dramatic, dynamic solutions.

Not showing all your cards can also be a tactical advantage. Know that the self-assurance and skill of Rogue Justice Warriors are transparent as others observe their poise and presence. Recall how in Chapter 2, we discussed the Vikings using the berserker technique to win many battles before they even began. Successful Rogue Justice Warriors allow everyone to see unerringly what is represented by their persona. The RJW understands that controlling the personal aura that others perceive is to their benefit.

There is a fine line between confidence and cockiness; gutsiness and foolishness; decisiveness and impulsivity; mental ruggedness and arrogant aggression. Contemporaries appreciate that Rogue Justice Warriors are authentically heroic, living the balance between standing above the multitudes and standing within the masses. Fighting fiercely for what is right will likely foster either respect or disdain, but **why** the warrior chooses to fight will be readily apparent to any observer.

**Rogue Scorecard**

The following 10 real-world scenarios are designed to help assess your individual level of rogue-ness. There is no clear-cut right or wrong answer in this rogue-ness quiz. Choose the option that your instinct tells you is best. As you study the situations, be completely honest in your responses. You may find that your preferred response to the scenario is clearly represented by one of the answer choices. Or, you may find that your answer is not included as an option. Either way, choose the response that best represents the course of action you envision yourself taking if you had to address the predicament.

**Question # 1**. You are an executive in a large nonprofit organization. One of your direct reports (an all-star performer) publicly refuses to verify a blatant lie told by the Chairman of the Board. Embarrassed, the Chairman is furious with the star performer, and makes the statement that "She (subordinate) will never go anywhere or get anything as long as I am in charge of this organization." Several months later, the top performer requests attendance at a high-level conference that will boost her profile, increase her pay potential, and put her in good standing for a promotion. The formal approval process for attendance at the conference requires consent from the Chairman of the Board. As the supervisor of the all-star performer, you decide to:

    A. **Deny the request because you already know the position of the Board Chairman**
    B. **Independently approve the request and send the em-**

*ployee to the conference because you believe it will benefit her and the organization*
*C. Approach the Chairman of the Board seeking formal approval of the request*
*D. Tell the employee that you will consider her request next year after the Chairman of the Board has a chance to settle down*

**Question # 2**. You are a high-level manager in a large manufacturing company. The CEO calls a mandatory emergency meeting off all executives. During the meeting, the CEO reveals that the company is in decline and faces severe financial obstacles. The CEO provides details about employee lay-offs, plus a 15% pay cut for all line employees that will take effect in 1-week. The Vice President tells managers that it is their job to "spin" the bad news to their direct reports. She directs all managers to soften and sugarcoat the message so that the impact of the news does not seem so devasting. You:

*A. Object during the meeting, telling all (CEO and Vice President included) that you do not agree with the directive to spin the information (lie) to employees*
*B. Gently spin the message to employees as ordered*
*C. Completely ignore the directive. Employees will find out on their own soon enough*
*D. Tell direct reports the truth – let them decide how they wish to process the information*

**Question # 3**. You supervise 20 employees at an off-site location. The employees are required to report to the office prior to commencement of their daily tasks. You notice that one employee is absent from the office for hours at a time in the middle of the day. During a private inquiry, the employee tells you that he has a severely disabled son, and that he (employee) must be home with that child for 4-hours in the middle of the day until his wife gets home to take over. You tell the employee:

*A. He must quit babysitting his son on work time*
*B. Continue doing what he is doing, the company is glad to help with the care of his disabled son*
*C. He must use leave/vacation time while he is not on-the-clock if he chooses to continue the current care plan for his son*
*D. He can work alternative hours (make up the lost time) if he works a full 8-hours everyday*

**Question # 4.** You are a rising sophomore on the varsity softball team at your school. After practice one afternoon, your friend and teammate confesses to you that the head coach has been making lewd remarks toward her, and that he is sending inappropriate texts to her phone. Your teammate is upset, but tells you that she does not wish for you to tell anyone because it would likely end her career and quash her chances of winning a college scholarship. Upon learning of this quandary, you decide to:

*A. Anonymously report the bad behavior to the school athletic director*
*B. Comply with the wishes of your teammate and do nothing*
*C. Approach an assistant coach seeking help*
*D. Challenge the head coach straightaway*
*E. Tell your parent about the dilemma*

**Question # 5.** As a corrections officer in a major city, your job is to process incoming prisoners to the jail. One night, a deputy brings a highly intoxicated male into the processing bay. The prisoner is unable to stand or walk without assistance. You witness the deputy struggling to remove the detainee from his vehicle, so you proceed in that direction to help. You see the arresting deputy strike the prisoner several times in the face with his fists, then you witness the deputy deliberately sling the handcuffed arrestee hard onto the concrete floor face first. You observe that the prisoner is now bleeding from wounds to his face and head. The arresting deputy tells your co-workers that the prisoner's injuries were caused when he accidently fell. You decide to:

A. Remain silent
B. Help the prisoner as best that you can by cleaning him up
C. Challenge the arresting deputy, demanding that he tell the truth regarding the detainees' injuries
D. Contact the Sheriff anonymously thru a public hotline
E. Reveal the truth to the jail intake supervisor after the arresting deputy leaves

**Question # 6**. You are a supervisor in a prominent law firm. You and 5 of your co-workers attend a Nascar race out-of-town. All except the designated driver, are enjoying a few alcoholic drinks on the trip to the track, at the race, and on the way home. By the end of the day, one overindulging co-worker is drunk, belligerent, and argumentative. As a supervisor, you tell the drunk co-worker that he will be given a ride home, and that he is not to drive. Upon arrival at the location where your vehicles are parked, the drunk co-worker runs to his vehicle, fires it up, and quickly drives away before he can be stopped. You then:

A. Call 911 and report your co-worker as a drunk driver
B. Report the bad behavior to the law firm hierarchy the next day
C. Hope that he makes it home safely as there is nothing that can be done at this point
D. Direct two fellow co-workers to follow and escort the drunk driver to his home
E. Quietly discipline the drunk employee upon his return to work without notifying superiors

**Question # 7**. You have been employed at the **Get Well Soon** Dermatology Center for nearly a year. The center is owned and operated by two well-known, hardworking, dermatologists. The Doctor's are well respected in their field, and were educated at highly regarded medical institutions. However, over time, you notice that the Doctors consistently disregard professional standards for routine services. Due to suspicions, you begin to examine patient medical records. Your investigation reveals that the Doctors are falsely diagnosing patients with skin cancer and then administering expensive and unnecessary drug treatments to inflate medical center revenue. You decide that you should:

    A. *Quit the job immediately to preserve your reputation*
    B. *Report your findings to law enforcement*
    C. *Confront the Doctors with the data that you have discovered*
    D. *Contact State Medical Board*
    E. *Do nothing, revealing the damning information could cause you to be unemployed*

**Question # 8**. You have been a computer intelligence analyst at a state security agency for 8-years. You become aware that your employer is conducting illegal surveillance programs. State government, without a warrant, is collecting, storing, and using private cell phone data in violation of Federal law. When you attempt to address the illicit nature of the program with your supervisor, you are told that it will be in your best interest to forget what you saw and keep quiet. You decide to:

    A. *Remain silent to protect your job*
    B. *Contact an attorney seeking self-protection*
    C. *Blow the whistle by reporting your findings to well-known tv reporter*
    D. *Confront the political appointee who heads the State agency*
    E. *Quit the job and seek employment elsewhere*

**Question # 9**. On your way thru a grocery store parking lot, you witness one vehicle strike another. As it attempted to back out, the left front of the striking vehicle struck the right rear of an unoccupied parked vehicle. Both vehicles have damage from the incident. The driver of the striking vehicle stops, gets out, and inspects the damage to both automobiles. The striking driver then re-enters his vehicle and begins to drive away. You decide that you should:

    A. *Chase down the fleeing driver to get him to stop*

B. Record the license plate and description of the offender and his car
C. Ignore it, not my business
D. Call law enforcement to anonymously report the hit-and-run accident
E. Leave a note on victim's windshield, and report incident to store management

**Question # 10.** You and Terri are close friends. Terri has been the top salesperson in your retail company for 3-years running. She seemingly has the magic touch. Her commissions are consistently higher than average, and she has once again received the coveted employee of the year bonus. One day, purely by accident, you discover that Terri is letting friends and family take items from the store without paying for the merchandise. She consistently fails to ring up (underreports) sales to friends, while family members regularly enjoy a five-finger discount. While observing Terri over a two-weeks period, you realize that the employee pilfering is likely more than a $1000.00 dollars per month. You decide that you should:

A. *Tell your supervisor that you suspect Terri of theft*
B. *Call law enforcement to file a report*
C. *Admonish Terri, inform her that you know what she is up to*
D. *Preserve your friendship by staying quiet*
E. *Covertly report incident to store management so that they can begin an investigation*

## How Rogue Are You?

How did you do on the rogueometer assessment? Your responses to the scenarios that you just completed provide a solid gauge of your Rogue Justice Warrior tendencies. These everyday dilemmas—while not overly complex—serve as a revealing warm-up to assess your level of rogueness. This self-scored tool offers a quick snapshot of whether you are *Non-Rogue, Somewhat Rogue, Rogue*, or a *Raging Rogue Justice Warrior*.

If you believe you have what it takes to be a **Rogue Justice Warrior,** visit [www.RogueJusticeWarrior.com](www.RogueJusticeWarrior.com). On the website, you can complete an in-depth, intensive, online Rogue Justice Warrior assessment. Our online instrument will score the results of your test, and display your calculated level of rogueness. Those who earn the distinction of **Raging Rogue Justice Warrior** will receive a certificate worthy of prominent display. Good luck, let's see what you're made of!

*"Thank my lucky stars to be living' here today, cause the flag still stands for freedom, they can't take that away. And I'd gladly stand up next to you and defend her still today, cause there ain't no doubt I love this land. God bless the USA"*

**Lee Greenwood**

# Conclusion

*Rogue Justice* represents influential, daring, and courageous engagement taken to reverse abuse, eradicate unfairness, or overturn inequality. A Rogue Justice Warrior acts according to hearty internalized principles, prioritizing what is best for all, versus what is best for them individually. They defiantly stand up for justice regardless of costs.

Courage, resilience, and boldness exemplifies the Rogue Justice Warrior. Taking gutsy action requires chutzpah. The ethical and respectable rogue does not dodge conflict, they scuffle daringly when they believe in a cause. Reputable rogues refuse to allow fear to inhibit their desire to make a difference.

Bravery, intensity, and valor pour out of the Rogue Justice Warrior's veins. Frequently the caretaker of civil liberty, they relish warfare when they feel that freedoms are at stake. They delight in going beyond boundaries when required to drive needed transformation.

Rogue Justice Warriors take clever, well thought out gambles, practice straight talk, and never concede an ounce of integrity. Their praiseworthy patriotism, combined with cunning and charisma, make them daunting adversaries in any confrontation.

Rogue leaders rely on the rumblings of gut instinct. Some may call them eccentric, rabblerouser, renegade, or even mutineer, but they are the ones willing to do hard things that need to be done. Rogue Justice Warriors revolutionize the world because they are uncontrollable and believe that they can! Rogue Justice Warrior s are true heroes who valiantly stand up to scandalous abuses!

Our nation needs You, Rogue Justice Warrior, now more than ever! Personify the creed ***"When you're right, you fight"*** in every thought and deed! I challenge all readers to live and perform every minute of every day as a Rogue Justice Warrior! Do it for your family, do it for your country, do it for your neighbors, and do it for yourself! You will be glad that you did! Never stop until injustice is eradicated!

# ABOUT THE AUTHOR

**Steve Neal** – worked as a highly respected law enforcement officer in Virginia for more than 29-years. During his tenure he was fortunate to experience a wide range of assignments, which included Uniform Operations, Criminal Investigations, Covert Operations, Director of the Emergency Communications Center, Director of Training, Support Services Commander, and Inspector for the Office of Professional Standards. He has comprehensive knowledge about selection and development of a public safety workforce, expertise regarding covert investigations, and a special affinity for media relations.

Steve's distinguished law enforcement career includes many awards and commendations. He is proud of his reputation as a "Cop's cop," a leader who places the welfare of those under his command as his top priority. He is respected by those who have served with him, and has been a mentor and coach to many officers. Steve is well known as a man of strong values, straight talk, and true to his word. Rebelling against injustice since childhood, he embodies the doctrine, **"When You're Right You Fight,"** regardless of political consequences.

Steve was the architect of Public Safety University (PSU), a college degree partnership between the public safety community and the University of Richmond. More than two-hundred and fifty public safety officers obtained Bachelor and/or Master degrees through the PSU program under his leadership.

Co-founder and partner of the Leatherman & Neal public safety consulting team, Steve enjoyed providing leadership seminars for peace officers for more than a decade. In addition to his consultancy, he has worked as a media contributor, furnishing analysis, consultation, and crime commentary for local television

## ABOUT THE AUTHOR

broadcasters. Steve appeared as a law enforcement authority on the nationally syndicated television show *For My Man*.

Steve Neal is the author of the broadly praised book **Toxic Boss Blues,** and co-author **of Bearing Witness to Evil. Toxic Boss Blues** is a leadership book that explores the devastating cost of noxious supervisory mismanagement. **Bearing Witness to Evil** is a true crime book that features 15 prominent crime cases from Steve's career, and a fascinating *"Story Behind the Story"* segment for each incident.

Steve has appeared as a guest on many podcasts, and he has written several articles that have been published online by *Law Enforcement Today, Law Officer*, and *Police 1* magazines.

# Sources and Credits

Alexander, Kathy, www.legandsofamerica.com, 2022

Arden, Paul (Quote)

Bible: King James Version

Bible: New King James Version

Bible: New International Version

Donica, Adrienna and Biography.com Editors, www.biography.com/us-president/donald-trump, 2021

Elliot, Simon, www.historyhit.com), 2018

Farson, Dr. Richard, *Management of the Absurd*, 1999

Fordant, Christina, *Williams vs. Pennsylvania*,

Gaille, Louise, *15 Advantages and Disadvantages of the Jury System*, March 15, 2020, https://www.themarshallproject.org

Graham, Billy, (Quote)

Greenwood, Lee, *Proud to be an American,* 1984

Gross, Terry, *Pediatrician who exposed Flint water crisis*, 2018

Hamalainen, Pekka, 2022

Jackson, Andrew, (Quote)

Keay, Jack (Artistic depiction)

Kennedy, Robert (Quote)

Library of Congress, image of Donald Trump

Mark, Joshua, www.worldhistory.org, 2024

McCune, B.F. & Hart, Louis, *Wild West Magazine*, 1997

Merriam-Webster Dictionary

Neal, Steve, *When You're Right, You Fight*

Oxford English Dictionary

# SOURCES AND CREDITS

Owen, Jarus, *Who Are the Assyrians*? Live Science, 2016

Pierce, David Hyde (Quote)

Powers, Thomas, *The Killing of Crazy Horse*, 2010

Roosevelt, Theodore (Quote)

Shankar, Sri Sri Ravi (Quote)

Sitting Bull (Quote)

Smallwood, Karl, *The Truth About Gladiators and the Thumbs Up*, 2014

Tearle, Dr. Oliver: *A Summary and Analysis of Martin Luther King's Letter from Birmingham Jail*, 2024 www.interestingliterature.com

Tyson, Mike (Quote)

Wahra, Andreas (Artistic representation of Jesus Christ)

Wikimedia Commons

www.ar.inspiredpencil.com (Photo of Tiananmen Square Tank Man)

www.bbc.com

www.Biography.com

www.britannica.com

www.Civilrightsmuseum.org

www.Christianity.org

www.cnn.com

www.Dictionary.com

www.freedictionary.com

www.girlsunited.essence.com (Jordon Chiles photo)

www.Harriet-Tubman.org Harriet Tubman Historical Society, 2024

www.history.com Editors Feb. 20, 2024

www.historycollection.com

www.historyhit.com

www.Historynet.com

www.Legendsofamerica.com

www.legaldictionary.com

www.Merriam-Webster.com

www.militaryhistorynow.com , Military History Now, 2019

www.monahannaattisha.com

www.NationalSCLU.org

www.NationalWW2museum.org

www.NBC.com

www.nebme.org/reparative-justice

www.nps.gov National Historical Park, 2024

www.Politifact.com

www.pattonhq.com Charles M. Province, The Patton Society, 2024

www.romanempirehistory.com, 2023

www.Smithsonianmag.com

www.themarshallproject.com)

www.thoughtco.com

www.Today.com

www.trumpwhitehousearchives.gov

www.USA.com

www.USAToday.com

www.USMint.gov

www.vocabulary.com

www.wallpaperaccess.com (Photo of Scales of Justice)

www.Winstonchurchill.org

www.Whitehouse.gov (Theodore Roosevelt)

# SOURCES AND CREDITS

www.wikipedia.org

www.winstonchurchill.org

www.Youtube.com (Photo of Honey Badger)